The Bo...
Bi...

THE BOOK OF Snooker and Billiards Quotations

Eugene Weber & Clive Everton

STANLEY PAUL

LONDON

Stanley Paul & Co Ltd

An imprint of Random House (UK) Limited
20 Vauxhall Bridge Road, London SW1V 2SA

Random House Australia (Pty) Ltd
20 Alfred Street, Milsons Point, Sydney 2061

Random House New Zealand Ltd
18 Poland Road, Glenfield, Auckland 10

Random House South Africa (Pty) Ltd
PO Box 337, Bergvlei 2012, South Africa

First published 1993

Copyright © Eugene Weber and Clive Everton 1993
Illustrations © Stanley Paul 1993

The right of Eugene Weber and Clive Everton to be identified as the
authors of this work has been asserted in accordance
with the Copyright, Designs and Patents Act, 1988

Set in Times by SX Composing Ltd, Rayleigh, Essex

Printed and bound in Great Britain by
Mackays of Chatham plc, Chatham, Kent

A catalogue record for this book is available upon
request from the British Library

ISBN 0 09 177620 1

Illustrations by Robin Bouttell

Contents

Acknowledgements   *7*

Frontispiece   *8*

 1 147   *9*

 2 Aggravation   *14*

 3 Audience Participation   *21*

 4 Billiards   *23*

 5 Criticism   *30*

 6 Cues   *31*

 7 Distractions   *36*

 8 Drugs   *38*

 9 Etiquette   *41*

10 Exhibitions   *43*

11 Getting Old   *45*

12 Health   *46*

13 Hustling   *48*

14 Hype   *49*

15 Inspiration   *50*

16 Losing   *52*

17 Luck   *58*

18 Managing   *59*

19 Marriage   *64*

20 Media   *65*

21 Misbehaving   *67*

22 *Money*	*69*
23 *Nicknames*	*72*
24 *Oddballs*	*77*
25 *Playing*	*85*
26 *Pool*	*98*
27 *The Powers That Be*	*100*
28 *Practice*	*102*
29 *Pressure*	*104*
30 *Referees*	*110*
31 *Retirement*	*112*
32 *Self-Image*	*113*
33 *Sponsorship*	*118*
34 *Success*	*119*
35 *Television*	*121*
36 *Television Commentators*	*125*
37 *Winning*	*136*
38 *Women Players*	*140*
39 *World Championships*	*145*
40 *Youth*	*150*
41 *Final Word*	*154*
Index	*156*

Acknowledgements

The authors would like to express their gratitude to the following who have helped us to compile this collection.

Our thanks to Colin Webb, Editor-in-Chief of the Press Association, for permission to use the PA's Newspaper Cuttings Library. We would also like to thank Vivienne Dungate at PA.

The assistance of Julie Kane, chief archivist at Snooker Scene, was invaluable.

We would also like to record our thanks to James Weber; Jeff Care, Scott Harrison, Milli Pollard and June Sirc at the *Observer* newspaper; Stuart Dempster at Express Newspapers and Natalia Medvedeva.

Frontispiece

Well, we're all snookers at this game so we'd better just call it that.

Col. Sir Neville Chamberlain with what is probably the first quotation about snooker. It was Chamberlain who suggested that the game of billiards could be brightened by the introduction of coloured balls. A 'snooker' is army slang for a rookie at the Royal Military Academy.

1
147

It's nice to make a maximum in competition but I'm also disappointed that there is no money in it. There should be something. Where is Barry Hearn?

>JAMES WATTANA after his untelevised 147 at the World Masters in 1991.

I was thinking of a big money.

>IBID.

This is the one thing I wanted. I am still in a daze and my legs were like jelly on the last black. I was lucky John scattered the reds and they all kept clear of the cushions. But they still wanted potting.

>STEVE DAVIS on the first ever televised maximum in his match with John Spencer during the Lada Cars Classic in 1982.

I wanted to jump up in the air but I didn't know what to do. I shall remember it for a long time. Very exciting.

>IBID.

147 – That's my idea of Heaven.

>TITLE of record made by Alex Higgins. He bought 3500 copies of it.

No one can ever take this away from me.

>CLIFF THORBURN's reaction to his 147 in the 1983 Embassy World Championship.

147 – *That's my idea of Heaven*

I'D rather this one than the title.

>IBID.

I can't begin to explain how I feel. My father may have been with me somehow when I made the break. I had a good feeling all the way through it.

>JAMES WATTANA who was told of his father's death in a shooting incident in Bangkok shortly after compiling a maximum in the 1992 Pearl Assurance British Open.

WHEN the final black went in, the feeling of satisfaction was ample compensation for all those disappointments and lonely hours of practice which every sportsman has to go through before achieving a lifetime's ambition.

>REX WILLIAMS on the 147 he made in an exhibition match with Mannie Francisco in South Africa.

THE money doesn't worry me. It was just a good feeling to finally get a 147 in a tournament.

>WILLIE THORNE. He earned £6750 for his maximum but would have netted £50,000 had it been achieved during the televised stage of the 1987 Tennents UK Open.

WHEN I potted the green I was thinking of the Bahamas. When I potted the blue all I could see was pound notes.

>JOE JOHNSON who potted 15 reds, 15 blacks, the yellow, green, brown and blue but missed the pink during his attempt at a 147 in the 1987 Tennents UK Open.

How long have I been off the booze? That's easy – 27 days, three hours and 21 minutes.

>JIMMY WHITE after his 147 in the 1992 World Championship.

BEST of luck mate.

>JACK KARNEHM while commentating as Cliff Thorburn lined up the final black of his 147.

It's my proudest moment and nothing will ever rival it. For the first time I really believed I could be world champion.

> KIRK STEVENS after he made a maximum during his semi-final clash with Jimmy White in the 1984 Benson & Hedges Masters.

I couldn't believe how I felt. I was just enthralled in it, lost in it.

> IBID.

So I finally made it. I don't care if I never hit another ball.

> JOE DAVIS after he became the first player to make a break of 147 under match conditions on a standard table.

A maximum doesn't signify anything except a good performance. If you make a 147 or you win on the black you've still only won one frame. It doesn't tell the truth.

> FRED DAVIS.

Like a hole-in-one in golf, a maximum snooker break can only ever be an aimed-for fluke.

> JOHN SPENCER.

You don't need to be world champion if you have that under your belt.

> RAY REARDON on Cliff Thorburn's maximum.

People can always take the title off you, but nobody can take that first 147 away.

> CLIFF THORBURN.

It's the magic number: seven more
than black despair and that last black
has to be the hardest, he poises
his cue, and we all feel sick

with certainty: he won't make it.
That black is every job interview
we failed; every final step
we tripped on. It's every no

we heard when we needed to hear yes,
and it's going to happen again,
it's bound to. There's the contact: too late now.
It's poised on the lip; we all breathe in

and it's down, and everyone going mad,
because destiny's taken a day off
and we've won. His laughter radiates
out at the audience; they mirror love

back to him, and everyone wants
to hold him, touch him, touch the luck,
in case it's catching. He did it
for all of us; he put down the black

'147', a poem by Sheenagh Pugh, inspired by Kirk Stevens' maximum in the 1984 Benson & Hedges Masters.

2
Aggravation

I come from Shankill, you come from Coalisland. Next time you come back to Northern Ireland, I'll have you shot.

> ALEX HIGGINS to team-mate Dennis Taylor in an argument over the prize money for the highest break during the 1990 British Car Rental World Cup.

I wish to apologise for the remark made to Dennis Taylor, said in the heat of the moment, and which I now publicly retract. I very much regret my outburst.

> ALEX HIGGINS.

My final apology is to the people of the thirty-two counties of Ireland for any embarrassment caused to them.

> ALEX HIGGINS.

Oh yes – it looks well mannered. It's like Jane Austen – regulated hatred.

> CLIVE EVERTON, editor of *Snooker Scene*, during the 1981 Embassy World Championship.

So eventually, as we go to shake hands, I kick him right in the nuts.

> CLIFF THORBURN describing the breakdown of peace proposals between him and Alex Higgins.

The first time I met the Hurricane, I took an instant dislike to him. The second time I beat him up.

> CLIFF THORBURN.

SOMEONE threw a petrol bomb at him and he drank it.

>COMEDIAN Frank Carson on Alex Higgins.

GET going Eddie.
I would if you'd shut your big mouth.

>EXCHANGE of pleasantries between Eddie Charlton and a spectator.

I hate Steve Davis, but I respect him as a player.

>ALEX HIGGINS.

OF course we hate each other. We always have done, but I love playing against him.

>DAVIS on Higgins.

FRANKLY, I'd rather have a drink with Idi Amin.

>HIGGINS on Davis.

THAT's probably because Amin buys more rounds.

>DAVIS.

THEY like him because he makes shots look difficult merely by contorting his body.

>DAVIS on Higgins.

SOMETIMES when I'm playing, I look over at the other player and think 'God, I hate you', but when the match is over, it's over. It's a nice kind of aggressive attitude, and the thing is to find the right balance between that aggression and control.

>NEAL FOULDS.

I just said 'Thank you, Alex, would you make your way to the interview room.' Then he punched me in the stomach.

> COLIN RANDLE, press officer, describing an altercation with Alex Higgins during the 1990 Embassy World Championship.

IF you're a tiger, you mark your own ground. If someone intrudes on it you air your grievance.

> ALEX HIGGINS complaining that Tony Knowles was standing in his line during their meeting in the 1988 Benson & Hedges Masters.

How did you do that?
I believe you know my terms for tuition, Mr Reece.

> EXCHANGE between Melbourne Inman and Tom Reece following a fluke by Inman.

EXCUSE me, my Lord. But if you knew as much as I do about Inman you would have given Crippen the cup and sentenced Inman to death.

> TOM REECE to Lord Alverston, then president of the Billiards Association, as he presented the cup to Melbourne Inman who had just won the 1919 Billiards Championship. Earlier in the week Lord Alverston had sentenced Dr Crippen to death.

I got punched in the face in a fight – it wasn't the horse.

> ALEX HIGGINS explaining how he got a black eye.

THERE are people who would be willing to kill to take the world championship away from me. I'm the one that's here to kill and that's exactly what I intend to do.

> ALEX HIGGINS during the 1983 World Championship.

IF you were playing him at darts, you'd have one behind your ear before you'd picked your own off the board.

> MARTIN GRIFFITHS, Terry's father, on Alex Higgins.

I hope he doesn't go out of snooker because the only other job he would want is God's and that will take a bit of getting.

CLIFF WILSON on Barry Hearn.

I'M glad Higgins lost. He's dragged the game down.

JOHN PULMAN on Alex Higgins' defeat by Eddie Charlton in the 1973 World Championship.

I like John. I bought him a birthday cake one year, you know. I think he was 147.

ALEX HIGGINS on Pulman.

WE don't get on. In fact I don't like him. But sometimes I wish I could be like him.

ALEX HIGGINS on Eddie Charlton.

HIGGINS likes to compare himself with poor George Best, but that is not right. He is more like Sid Vicious: a man in total subjection to his own personal myth.

JOURNALIST Simon Barnes.

I love it when something goes a little bit wrong. I need a bit of aggro to get my adrenalin going.

RAY REARDON.

THE last time he won a match a star appeared in the East.

JOHN PULMAN.

HELLO, I'm the devil.

ALLEGED remark by Alex Higgins to Stephen Hendry.

I need a bit of aggro to get my adrenalin going

WELL done Stephen, you were a bit lucky.

> HIGGINS' version of what he said.

UP your **** you ****

> HENDRY'S version of what Higgins said.

THE game is bigger than Higgins and I consider him to be a menace, not only to himself but to everyone around him. He must be removed from our midst.

> IAN DOYLE, Hendry's manager.

ALEX is a demented raving lunatic and sooner or later someone will be hurt by him. I can't even call him a man.

> IBID.

MR Higgins is not seriously hurt. He landed on his head.

> A POLICEMAN giving the good news after Alex Higgins left his girlfriend's flat through a first-floor window.

I must have been playing extremely well for someone to have made such a call.

> STEVE DAVIS reacting to the news that he had received a death threat during the 1983 Embassy World Championship.

YOU'D kill your own grandmother for two bob.

> ALEX HIGGINS to Willie Thorne in a row over a 'miss'.

WE have a saying in Wales that sums up Hearn. He is a big girl's blouse.

> CLIFF WILSON on Barry Hearn.

I used to know someone like Barry at school. His dad was rich and he was the only boy who could afford a football. If you didn't pass to him he would pick it up and go home.

IBID.

STEVE's mean. If he was in the Mafia, they'd get rid of him for being too rough.

ROBBO BRAZIER, Steve Davis's minder.

3
Audience Participation

CALL yourself a pro, you couldn't pot a plant.

> COMMON remark from hecklers.

THE only trouble is I haven't got a machine gun.
Don't you worry, Terry. We can fix that up for you.

> EXCHANGE between Terry Griffiths and a member of the audience during an exhibition in Northern Ireland when Griffiths was preparing to play the machine-gun trick shot.

Do you think you can get in?
Well I could if the pockets were as big as your mouth.

> BANTER between Dennis Taylor and a spectator.

I didn't realise you're not supposed to shout 'Bravo' when the ball goes down the hole.

> SINGER Marianne Faithfull after being thrown out of a tournament for displaying excessive enthusiasm.

EXCUSE me, Mr Reardon, but do you know you're wearing odd socks?

> UNEXPECTED interjection from a spectator to Ray Reardon during the Pontins Open.

HEY John, get out of my way.

> SPECTATOR to Doug Mountjoy when he was playing Alex Higgins during the 1977 Super Crystalate United Kingdom Championships.

WHEN the gentleman has extinguished his bonfire, I'll resume.

MELBOURNE INMAN to a spectator who had struck a match during play.

POLL tax my bum.

SLOGAN on balloon worn by snooker's first streaker Christian Hennessey. The balloon was his only attempt at a cover-up.

4
Billiards

BILLIARDS is not like chess. In billiards you have to think.

>RUSSIAN saying.

To play billiards well is a sign of a misspent youth.

>HERBERT SPENCER, philosopher. Nowadays this quotation usually refers to snooker rather than billiards. Spencer claimed he heard it from someone else.

NOT enough balls.

>BBC producer Brian Wenham, explaining why billiards would not be suitable for television.

IT's a lonely business. We play each other occasionally. I go to John Barrie's house and we hammer each other. Nobody watches.

>JACK KARNEHM.

IT is truly the game beautiful.

>IBID.

BILLIARDS demands so much care, it doesn't fit into the modern world.

>IBID.

SNOOKER, you go to see blood, guts and tears. In billiards you go to see the artistry. It is the only game where you control the three balls. In snooker you control one; the other dives into the pocket.

>IBID.

WITH billiards you are talking about technique and finesse. Snooker is more crash, bang.

>   NORMAN DAGLEY.

I'VE never understood what motivates billiard players. Can you imagine that – you get dressed up in your lounge suit in the afternoon, you go on, you break off and then you sit there for the rest of the afternoon. You don't get a shot. Then you go back to the hotel and change from your lounge suit into your evening suit, and you go back and still don't get a shot. And the next morning you get up and shave and go back in the hall and the guy's still at the table. That would drive me to distraction.

>   ALEX HIGGINS.

IF you played snooker you were considered an extrovert.

>   NORMAN DAGLEY.

THEY'LL stand for a lot of things, but they'll never stand for this.

>   WILLIE SMITH, world billiards champion in the 1920s, reacting to billiard players' attempts to promote snooker as a public entertainment.

A man who wants to play billiards must have no other ambition. Billiards is all.

>   E. V. LUCAS.

LET's to billiards.

>   WILLIAM SHAKESPEARE, *Antony and Cleopatra*.

I'D like to be the Gene Tunney of the billiards world.

>   JOE DAVIS.

BILLIARDS, this most genteel, cleanly and ingenious game.

>   CHARLES COTTON, poet.

Let's to billiards

THE billiard table is the paradise of the ball.

ALFRED E. CRAWLEY, anthropologist.

BILLIARDS is very similar to snooker except there are only three balls and no one watches it.

STEVE DAVIS.

WOMEN really shoot billiards as well as men. We just miss more often.

DOROTHY WISE, pool player.

INDIANS are perhaps the only people who can still place the austere skills of billiards above the gaudy promiscuity of snooker.

ERIC SILVER, journalist.

. . . a billiard player of average ability can always turn his hand to playing quite a good game of snooker, whereas a fair snooker player rarely can turn his hand to playing a good game of billiards.

JACK KARNEHM.

UP, all of us, and to billiards.

SAMUEL PEPYS, diaries.

AFTER dinner to billiards, where I won an angel.

IBID.

The billiard sharp whom any one catches,
His doom's extremely hard –
He's made to dwell
In a dungeon cell,
On a spot that's always barred.
And there he plays extravagant matches,
In fitless finger stalls,
On a cloth untrue,
With a twisted cue,
And elliptical billiard balls.

WILLIAM S. GILBERT, lyricist and dramatist.

As smooth as a billiard ball.

BEN JONSON.

It is a beautiful game, with its own rhythm and satisfactions.

FRED DAVIS.

Billiards requires sweetness of touch, delicacy of operation, skill in planning and infinite variety.

FRED DAVIS.

The difference between billiards and snooker is that between chess and draughts. Second chances in top-class billiards are very, very rare.

LESLIE DRIFFIELD.

To watch the red ball eternally running up and down the central line of the table day in and day out, week in and week out, for years, was, sooner or later, bound to drive any player stark, staring mad.

COMMENT from unnamed player at the time of Australian George Gray's nervous breakdown. Gray's speciality was to play in off the red into a middle pocket and bring the red back from the top cushion into a position from which he could do it again.

This gentle game of science.

GEOFFREY GREEN, journalist.

Mark you, I found a greater poetic satisfaction in billiards.

JOE DAVIS.

I'm not going East after all. I find that billiards is better than all your doctors and I'm staying here.

MARK TWAIN.

I'd sooner have a game of billiards any day than go to the pictures. Billiards is a man's game; anyone can go to the pictures if they like. I go myself sometimes – when I can't find anyone to play billiards with, which is not often.

ROLAND FOXLEY, fourteen, speaking in 1937.

Children of righteous pre-war parents were brought up to fear God and snooker and honour the King and billiards.

DAVID HUNN, journalist.

The better the quality of billiards, the worse television it made.

ANONYMOUS.

To be good at billiards is more difficult because I don't know what to do.

DOUG MOUNTJOY.

If you don't play billiards, you lose all touch for the game.

DENNIS TAYLOR.

It was a common if somewhat exaggerated complaint, when Walter Lindrum, the great Australian billiards player, was hunched over the table making endless runs of nursery cannons, that a spectator could watch a whole session and never see his face.

CLIVE EVERTON.

A man does not go to perdition through handling a billiard cue, any more than he is saved by sitting on a library or kitchen committee.

RUDYARD KIPLING.

The most unkindest cut of all.

MR J. C. BISSET, then chairman of the BACC, on the decision to remove the billiard table used by Mary Queen of Scots on the night before her execution. Following the execution her head was wrapped in the cloth from the table.

Billiards is the game – snooker is a spectacle.

JOE DAVIS.

I think that the billiard ball so cleanly geometric in form and so ringingly clear in colour against the matt green of the baize must have appealed to my aesthetic sense in contrast to the fustiness of the Slade classroom.

ARTIST Ben Nicholson.

5
Criticism

I don't think working for a living has ever been highly regarded in this country. We have always preferred to inherit money or to have some strange knack like playing snooker. Even the Great Train Robbers got a grudging respect. To say that you have earned large sums of money has always brought a great deal of criticism.

> SIR JOHN EGAN, then chairman of Jaguar plc.

If snooker cannot stand controversy and face criticism, snooker does not deserve to be in the place it is today.

> CLIVE EVERTON.

6
Cues

OH my baby. It's sleeping next to me tonight. I'll never leave it alone again. It's an unbelievable relief. I had to think I might never see it again. I hope this cue will last out my career.

> STEPHEN HENDRY responding to the return of his stolen cue.

MY only reaction was 'God, my cue's broken.' It sounds terrible, but I just had to open that case before looking after him.

> STEVE DAVIS'S reaction to being involved in a road accident which trapped his driver.

I'D lost my cue and I'd lost my confidence. I was walking wounded. I was easy meat for anybody.

> ALEX HIGGINS.

IF you pick up the cue as if you were going to clout somebody over the head, the chances are you will grip it in about the right position for snooker.

> JOHN SPENCER.

TAKE everything I've got, including the wife, but leave my cue behind.

> RAY REARDON.

ONE player, one cue.

> SAYING.

*Oh my baby. It's sleeping next to me tonight.
I'll never leave it alone again*

SOME of these idiots have changed their cues and have never been able to play since. Me, I've had mine for fifty years. It's stuck together with dirt. It was given to me by Joe; he just gave it to me and I've played with it ever since.

>FRED DAVIS.

I joined the butt of one with the top of another. It's the happiest marriage I've seen in my life.

>ALEX HIGGINS.

IT's an extension of my right arm.

>RAY REARDON.

A lot of people are using two-piece cues nowadays. Alex Higgins hasn't got one because they don't come with instructions.

>STEVE DAVIS.

IT was very nerve-racking – I felt like a surgeon doing a brain operation. I broke out in a sweat when I had to cut it in half.

>CUE maker John Parris describing his feelings when changing Steve Davis's cue from a one-piece to a two-piece.

IN the nineteenth century 'cue' could also mean to swindle on credit, but I'm sure that has nothing to do with snooker.

>RAY REARDON.

I felt as if I had been bereaved.

>RAY REARDON after his cue was damaged.

UNTIL I saw the appeal I did not realise how much the cue means to you. I thought that you probably gave away the cue you used each time as a souvenir. Please accept my apologies for the suffering I have caused you.

>   NOTE attached to Ray Reardon's cue after it was returned to him by someone who had stolen it during Reardon's tour of South Africa.

IT has been to me what Excalibur was to King Arthur, the magic sword given to the ancient British hero of the sixth century by the Lady of the Lake, to ensure his immunity to severe wounds and loss of blood. Joe Davis was the snooker rock from whom I drew it and it has served me faithfully as well as any friend.

>   RAY REARDON.

The Fountain Pen Cue.

>   A miniature cue with tip produced by Alec Brown in his match with Tom Newman in 1938 when Brown found the cue ball in an awkward position among the pack of reds.

A pen is not a cue. It is something alien to the game and the fact that this one had a cue-tip on the end did not convert it into a cue.

>   REFEREE Charles Chambers ruling on the incident. He awarded a foul stroke against Brown.

A billiard cue, as recognised by the Billiards Association and Control Council, shall be not less than 3 ft in length and shall show no substantial departure from the traditional and general shape and form.

>   THE BACC's definition of a cue following the Fountain Pen incident.

IT had more tips than a head waiter.

>   QUIP about unreliable cues.

A good cue will need respect rather than regular attention during its life.

JACK KARNEHM.

You're never alone with a cue.

ALEX HIGGINS.

It's a weapon and a crutch to me.

IBID.

7
Distractions

I never buy them a drink. I never buy them a meal. I never dance with them. The only thing I offer them – apart from myself – is a lift home. And it works – every night of the week and sometimes several times a night.

>   TONY KNOWLES.

THERE is always someone wanting to buy me a drink. There is always some woman who is chasing you around. It is not easy to be a saint.

>   ALEX HIGGINS.

I think it's a great idea to talk during sex, as long as it's about snooker.

>   STEVE DAVIS.

I said no to Tony Knowles.

>   SLOGAN on T-shirt after Knowles told the *Sun* newspaper that he rated girls, not out of ten, but out of two – those who say yes and those who say no.

WHEN I tell the birds I'm a great potter, they know what I mean.

>   ALEX HIGGINS.

IF I found him with another woman there would be Mercedes sports car wheelmarks right up the front of his shirt – and hers. I know there are groupies and there's always a chance of something happening. I'm not the type to sit and worry about it – I'd just kill when I found out.

AVRIL VIRGO, wife of John.

IF this girl tries to come between Stephen and the world title, then she'll have to go.

IAN DOYLE on Stephen Hendry's long-time girlfriend Mandy Tart.

THE highest single bet I ever laid was £40,000 on one horse. It was like playing with Monopoly money and sometimes I couldn't even remember the names of the horses I was backing.

WILLIE THORNE.

I remember during one tournament, I'd backed a horse running in the 2.30 and actually looked up, before taking a crucial shot, at a friend in the audience. I'd arranged beforehand for him to give me the thumbs up if the horse won. It had. I was so elated I went on to win the next three frames.

IBID.

I'M going to be a professional snooker player rather than a professional gambler.

IBID.

8
Drugs

I am a cocaine addict. At first I was hooked just mentally. But now it has a total physical hold over me.

KIRK STEVENS, 1985.

MANY, many times I have sat in my hotel room in England and begged God for the police to come and knock the door in and find me because they were the only people who could help me – who would force me to get help.

IBID.

'PLEASE God,' I prayed, 'I've lost my soul. Please see me back to my soul.'

IBID.

I want the kids to know just how awful this drug is. The glamour that surrounds its image sickens me. It doesn't do anything but destroy – like it's very nearly destroyed me.

IBID.

I would like to see it banned. No one was allowed to smoke in the old days. It's well known I used to take beta blockers but a top medical man told me the greatest steadier of them all is nicotine.

REX WILLIAMS.

So many leading players seem to be taking beta blockers on medical advice that the only solution would appear to be to make it a condition of entry.

ALISON NOVICK in a letter to *Snooker Scene*.

THE trouble is that if players are convinced that beta blockers can help them they'll want them and soon every Tom, Dick and Harry will be on them. My doctor said he would prescribe beta blockers for me if I wanted but the day I need anything to help me play snooker is the day I give up.

FRED DAVIS.

IF you stop people with medical reasons for taking them it will be like stopping somebody with poor eyesight from wearing spectacles.

REX WILLIAMS on beta blockers.

SNOOKER is not an Olympic sport but it should, of course, have Olympic ideals.

CLIVE EVERTON.

IT is for snooker to decide whether it is a sport or an entertainment. If it is an entertainment it can decide to be free of ethical considerations of fair play. If it is a sport, normal sporting practice should apply.

SIR ARTHUR GOLD, chairman of the Sports Council's Drug Abuse Group.

HOWEVER important the use of beta blockers may be for the relief of certain medical conditions, the effect on sporting performance gives the player a significant drug-induced advantage. That is tantamount to cheating. Neal Foulds and other players under the influence of beta blockers should withdraw from the competition and stay away from the tables until they are fit to compete.

COLIN MOYNIHAN MP, then Minister for Sport.

To me it was simple: take drugs or die.

NEAL FOULDS.

I am not on drugs myself and I don't know of any snooker player who is. If they want to test me for rabies they are more than welcome.

ALEX HIGGINS.

THE photographers were all in there flashing.

IAN DOYLE describing the scene when Alex Higgins insisted on using a public toilet to provide a sample for a drug test.

9
Etiquette

IN the old days I had to wear starched cuffs and shirt front before being allowed to play. Those were times when aristocracy and royalty played the game. We cued up in cathedral-like rooms where a cough could send a man to Coventry.

JOE DAVIS.

SNOOKER is a game of high etiquette and good manners. I find that appealing.

DENE O'KANE.

I'M very fond of all sports but I'm a quiet sportsman. I'm fond of snooker because it's quiet and delicate. In a sense I like the politeness of it.

TED LOWE.

WHAT does irritate me, though, is not long hair, or bleached jeans and suede boots, or ragged pullovers and baggy trousers. They're all right in their place, but their place is not at the billiard table.

EDITORIAL in *Billiards & Snooker*, September 1971.

HIGGINS' dress (or lack of it), his behaviour when he is losing, his general demeanour, all bring the game into disrepute. It is awful for him to be called the 'People's Champion'. We too are people; he is not our champion. He gave himself this unearned and undeserved title.

    MRS I. E. DIFFLEY in a letter to *Snooker Scene*.

It's a gentleman's game at heart. Contestants are nicely dressed. It's played in an affable manner. There's no violence. It's a nice game. And, yes, I think it's artistic.

    RAY REARDON.

10
Exhibitions

WHERE's the table?
We thought you'd bring it with you.

> CONVERSATION between Fred Davis and an exhibition organiser.

I also felt like I was stealing. Where I was brought up every shot was for money – my own money. Suddenly here I was being paid. Just for turning up.

> KIRK STEVENS.

WHO called the organiser a ****?
Who called the **** an organiser?

> JOHN PULMAN failing to act as a peacemaker during an altercation before an exhibition.

I knew things couldn't be going too well when I saw the organiser in a gorilla suit going up and down the prom selling tickets.

> DOUG MOUNTJOY on an exhibition engagement in Rhyl.

ARE you the snooker player?
No I'm the ****ing chimney sweep.

> JOHN PULMAN arriving tuxedoed, cue case in hand, for a club exhibition.

I'VE cleared the reds. Where are the bloody colours?

> MELBOURNE INMAN knocking down a row of red lamps as he drove erratically away in his car.

I was counting on John with his vast experience of being pissed to save the day.

> CLIFF THORBURN recalling that he and John Pulman had been entertained too royally during an exhibition in Australia.

11
Getting Old

You can't defend against age, you can only come to terms with it.

>   FRED DAVIS.

It's a young man's game now. You can hang in there for five furlongs then they pot you off the table.

>   RAY REARDON.

Middle-aged snooker players are the Micawbers of the sporting world. They are always hoping that something will happen to their style of play which will make them a black or two better.

>   FRED DAVIS.

Kirk isn't the player he was. But then, neither am I.

>   ALEX HIGGINS on beating Kirk Stevens in the qualifiers for the 1993 Embassy World Championships.

The lads who beat me all had a good safety game, and when they had a difficult pot they knocked it in, not just once or twice, but almost every time.

>   REX WILLIAMS.

12
Health

BREAK up long spells of viewing by moving your head from side to side and roll your eyes. Better still stretch your eye muscles by looking out the window.

> MURIEL WALL, secretary of the British Migraine Association, on how to avoid headaches from watching too much snooker on television.

THE whole body is gently exercised and the mind refreshed in an activity where skill and chance are finely balanced.

> *PULSE*, the doctors' newspaper, extolling the virtues of playing billiards and snooker. In Victorian times doctors often prescribed a game for those of nervous disposition.

I suppose I'm some sort of freak but alcohol has no effect on me.

> BILL WERBENIUK, who suffers from an inherited nervous illness which causes his arm to tremble. The only cure he found was to imbibe vast quantities of lager.

I don't do any social drinking whatsoever – when I'm through with playing, I'm through with drinking for that evening.

> IBID.

I was in New Zealand four years ago and spent a free day playing on a hotel table with my old pal John Spencer. To save bar staff any trouble I was ordering a crate of lager at a time. John and I played for twenty hours and during that time I never stopped drinking.

> IBID.

I am not going to die for snooker, but also I won't let them take away my living.

BILL WERBENIUK defending his use of beta blockers.

FROM now on, during challenge matches and exhibitions, I'll take my daily dose of Inderal and stick to a sensible fifteen lagers. That won't do me any harm.

IBID.

THERE's no other beta blocker that will do the job. I've been taking it [Inderal] for fifteen years and I don't remember myself winning the World Championship.

IBID.

I packed up smoking but I couldn't relax. Now I'm smoking again – only twenty a day – and I've given up jogging and I feel much happier.

TERRY GRIFFITHS.

I went to the optician and received the most disappointing piece of good news I have ever had. My eyes were OK.

CLIFF THORBURN.

BEER for breakfast – what kind of life is that?

BILL WERBENIUK.

BILL represents all the world's heavyweights who long to be heroes but haven't got the figure for it.

JANICE HALE on Bill Werbeniuk.

13
Hustling

A hustler is anyone who has to make a living.

NEW YORK FATS, pool player.

GETTING the feel of the table.

EUPHEMISM used by hustlers to describe a sudden improvement in their performance.

THE days of the hustler have disappeared now that the game has moved on to a bigger stage. It's an inevitable evolution. Snooker players are all the better for it, but the excitement has gone. The thrill of the raw duel where you lay down the challenge, back your judgement with pound notes and fight it out there and then. No fancy theatre, no television cameras, no dinner jackets and bow ties . . . just a cue, a bottle of gin, a packet of fags and a game.

ALEX HIGGINS.

14
Hype

STEVE Davis has arrived.

ADVERTISEMENT placed in the snooker press when Davis turned professional.

HE's held together by hype.

ANONYMOUS snooker journalist on Alex Higgins.

15
Inspiration

My early inspiration was John Spencer. I must have read his book *Spencer on Snooker* thirty or forty times.

> NEW Zealander Dene O'Kane. He borrowed the book so often from his local library that he was eventually allowed to keep it.

Without Frank Callan I would be nothing.

> DOUG MOUNTJOY after winning the 1988 Tennents UK Championship – his first title win in ten years. His return to form followed coaching sessions from Callan.

Be the guv'nor.

> BARRY HEARN's advice to Steve Davis.

After a match, whether I win or lose, I never fail to thank God. I need God's help. And if I play with that need I feel at peace. Of course, I must also try. If I close my eyes and say 'God help me' and do nothing myself, that is foolishness.

> MOHAMMED LAFIR, world amateur billiards champion in 1973.

You'll never get anywhere in snooker, lad.

> PE TEACHER John Walsh to Jimmy White.

My particular style is called the Knowledge. I meditate most mornings, concentrating on getting to my inner self. I find it helps me a great deal.

> DENE O'KANE.

PLAYERS should not be bound by principles generally laid down in previous books. If need be they should experiment and find out if they can achieve their objectives in other ways. What suits one player will not automatically suit another.

FRANK CALLAN.

I'VE always had the knack of spotting people's faults and correcting them.

IBID.

I'D ask you to pray for me but you're such a bad Catholic nobody would listen.

MANNIE FRANCISCO to Michael Ferreira before his game with Norman Dagley.

TAKE that bloody grin off your face.

JOE DAVIS to his brother Fred. It was the only advice he ever gave.

BEFORE the final session of his semi-final against Jimmy White, Higgins, back in his hotel room, opened the Bible at the Acts of the Apostles. Then, for the last two frames of the match, he had a small gold Sacred Heart in his mouth, sent by a well-wisher in Dublin. None of the millions watching on TV could have guessed that the man who put their hearts in their mouths was experiencing just that himself in such a tangible way. 'I've got no bias, for I'm quite prepared to put the Heart in my mouth to bring me luck.'

JANICE HALE.

I had a drink and I were champion.

JOHN DUNNING, fifty-six, who is normally a non-drinker while playing, after winning his semi-final match in the 1984 Yamaha International Masters.

16
Losing

I'M just a born loser.

> TONY MEO after losing in the first round of the 1984 World Championships.

HE played all right, I suppose, but it was all the balls running against me in the first session that did me in. He's a talented player but I wouldn't say he is the best player in the world, even though the rankings would seem to prove it.

> DEAN REYNOLDS taking it like a man after being beaten 10–0 by Steve Davis in the final of the 1989 Rothmans Grand Prix.

YOU can't judge a player on one match. There are twenty players like him at my club. It will be interesting to see if he's still playing on the circuit in three years' time or down the Job Centre.

> DEAN REYNOLDS again taking it like a man after losing to rookie Jason Weston in the 1991 Pearl Assurance Open.

I'M disappointed but not bitterly.

> STEVE DAVIS on his 6–2 defeat by John Parrott in the 1990 Benson & Hedges Masters.

I got the message. I got ran over. It's scary when you look down your cue and see a nightmare.

> KIRK STEVENS after losing in the 1986 Embassy World Championship.

It's scary when you look down your cue and see a nightmare

TERRY Griffiths once said that there's a kind of beauty in defeat, all that working and striving and people feeling sorry when you fail. I know what he means but I can't pretend I like it.

STEVE DAVIS.

I played like a slow puncture. I started badly and got progressively worse. Even if I'd got into a couple of games in the last session I wouldn't have known what to do – I'd have needed a diagram.

JOHN PARROTT after losing to Steve Davis in the 1989 Embassy World Championship final.

I would have won if he hadn't turned up.

CLIFF WILSON on his defeat by Steve Davis in the 1988 Rothmans Grand Prix.

STEVE played strong, solid snooker. He did me like a kipper. I stuck to the honey and the vitamin pills but I still got stuffed.

ALEX HIGGINS after losing 16–5 to Steve Davis in the 1983 Embassy World Championship.

THERE were times when I was losing that I thought, 'Do I need this?' Then I think of the money; it's money for old rope. I can't believe how well we get paid for doing something I enjoy.

NEAL FOULDS.

IT could only happen in this country. All of a sudden everybody loves me because I'm a loser.

STEVE DAVIS.

I'M disappointed but not dissipated.

ALEX HIGGINS on his defeat by Willie Thorne in the 1986 Dulux British Open.

THE hardest part is watching snooker on the box for the next fourteen days.

ALEX HIGGINS on his first-round defeat in the 1988 Embassy World Championship.

I hope nobody gets any silly ideas about me being some sort of pushover – a sort of constantly stuffed Parrott – because I'm as hard as anyone in the game. I'm a very dedicated player.

> JOHN PARROTT on his difficulties in winning finals.

AFTER the game he ordered me to stay away from his daughter and called off the church wedding we had been planning.

> NORMAN SKIDMORE, nineteen, on the consequences of beating his prospective father-in-law.

THE worst that can happen if you lose is that you lose.

> FRANK CALLAN.

IF I don't start well, I don't usually start at all.

> GARY OWEN.

WHEN I heard I was to play Hurricane Higgins I thought I might turn out to be a Tornado, but I finished up as a bit of wind.

> RON GROSS after losing 16–5 to Higgins in the 1972 World Championship.

I feel as if I have just been eaten.

> ALEX HIGGINS on his 5–0 defeat by Steve Davis in the 1987 Mercantile Credit Classic.

WE had a few drinks and then drove home. We'd been away a month and I was really looking forward to spending time back at the flat, but it was hell. We'd not had a bite to eat all day but we just wanted to climb into bed. He was as tense as a steel bar and he kept saying, 'I had the chances but I've blown it,' and there was no way we were going to sleep. There was not much of a loving scene going. We were both shattered, still playing the match. We had some more talk and then a cigarette and I kept thinking, 'A year's work and he's bloody well lost,' and in turn I was as mad as hell and then I was crying and then he seemed to drop off to sleep. Except that all the time he kept turning and kicking about and muttering and I thought, 'He's going through hell, poor bastard.' I never slept all night and at nine o'clock I got up and took all the washing to the launderette and did a load of shopping and ironed everything and when he got up he said, 'What the hell have you done all that for,' and I don't even know now. It's bloody dreadful when your man's lost and you try to help and he says, 'You don't know what you're talking about,' and you know it's true. When he says he feels right and he doesn't need practice you don't know whether to say, 'Get down to some hard work, you lazy sod,' or keep quiet and reckon he knows best. He loses and I've cried and he's been embarrassed and he's won and his friends have come round and I've felt cut off. It's there, inside him, the ability to be world champion and I want to bring it out and still make him feel it's all down to him. At the moment it's not happening. It's hell being the woman in the life of a snooker star, I can tell you.

ANONYMOUS snooker wife.

I feel totally gutted but it was a good scrap.

JIMMY WHITE on his 16–14 defeat by Steve Davis in the final of the 1987 Tennents UK Open.

HAD it not been a woman player I could have shrugged it off but I haven't recovered yet. I've never been so disappointed. Now I've got no confidence at all.

NEAL FOULDS attributing his defeat in the 1992 Benson & Hedges Irish Masters to losing to Allison Fisher in the previous week.

THERE is beauty in defeat.

TERRY GRIFFITHS.

I'M not one for the wet handshake and being nasty afterwards. But in private I can get really upset. If you don't get upset when you lose there's no point in playing – because you don't really want to win.

ALLISON FISHER.

ONE minute you're the best thing since sliced bread and everybody's taking a slice. It's my job to stop people passing the plate around.

STEVE DAVIS.

17
Luck

I have heard a few of the television commentators and some players say that Davis is lucky. Steve is not a lucky player, just a very, very good one.

TERRY GRIFFITHS.

PERHAPS the players who are saying I am lucky should go back to the practice table.

STEVE DAVIS.

18
Managing

A good manager should be a bit of an Al Capone figure. He's got to give his players a bit of heavy protection, from ponces who are after his money, from groupies who are looking for something else.

BARRY HEARN.

I'VE built the walls around my players so that they are different. They are encouraged to feel special and I hope they do.

IBID.

So I expect and accept jealousy and antipathy. There's nothing I can do better than be more successful and annoy a few more people.

IBID.

THEY are turning everything into a string of petty jealousies. Some of them even get on to their players and try to tell them how to play the game.

RAY REARDON on managers and agents.

MANAGING a snooker player is a bit like owning a racehorse. There are a lot of fees to pay and the only return is when the horse's name is in the frame. As with racehorses the true satisfactions are in the involvement and the nice people you meet along the way.

ANTHONY BRIDGE, former manager.

As soon as he walked in the door, Providence smiled on me.

BARRY HEARN on Steve Davis.

I see myself as an extension of the Welfare State. Cradle to grave. Everything they want, everything they need, they ring Barry.

    BARRY HEARN.

HE was losing to a guy who shouldn't even have been in the same club, never mind on the same table. He was only sixteen but I pinned him up against the wall and told him in no uncertain terms that if he didn't get his act together I was going to smash him. I said, 'If you cost me another grand, I'm going to knock your bloody head off.' I think he got the message.

    IAN DOYLE giving an example of the Glasgow School of Motivation as applied to Stephen Hendry.

IF you see an opening you have to make a dash for it. Everyone wants to exploit the potential. Isaac Newton was an entrepreneur. So was Pythagoras. Anyone who invents anything. Yes, money is important. Yet I'm not an extremely wealthy man. I don't do anything now that I didn't do ten years ago. The harder I have worked the better I have got but at the same time you can work with nothing to show for it at the end of the day. I have been fortunate. I believed in something that everyone also believed in as well.

    MIKE WATTERSON, once snooker's leading promoter.

WE lay on limos for our players and people to carry their cue cases, sort out the hotel suites . . . everything is organised and sanitised. I want to intimidate other players. I want people they play against to feel inferior.

    BARRY HEARN.

YOU can be the best manager in the world but that counts for nothing if your players aren't winners.

    BARRY HEARN.

THERE is nothing merciful in my business make-up. I don't expect it from others and I don't believe in it.

    NOEL MILLER-CHEEVERS, property developer, snooker manager and keen amateur player.

You're only as good as your last two or three deals so there's no room for softness.

IBID.

In snooker the players are tremendous as individuals, but sometimes they have funny ideas and tend to forget that a few years ago they were playing for buttons. They forget how much they owe me. One or two of them would like to screw me into the carpet for earning money from snooker but five years ago I gambled my neck doing it. What used to be a fifty-pound-a-night game is now worth £2000 a night. I do not earn half as much as I ought to.

MIKE WATTERSON.

If you know a good tailor, I have got a lot of holes in the back of my jacket. I just do not see the point in trying to kill off people who have served the game so well.

IBID.

My whole strategy revolves around discipline. If you don't have discipline, you have nothing.

IAN DOYLE.

It's easy. They give me the prize money and I give them their cues back.

BARRY HEARN on his relationships with his players.

We are an extension of the Welfare State. The idea is to take away everything other than the worries of playing. We'll pay all their household bills, their school fees, organise their holidays, their itineraries, their life, their car, their wives, everything. We try not to get involved in domestic battles. But if necessary we would.

IBID.

My whole strategy revolves around discipline. If you don't have discipline, you have nothing

Most of all though, I miss being involved with the people in the game. It is all right going about emptying gaming machines for a living but it is excruciatingly boring.

>   MIKE WATTERSON.

Many snooker managers are nothing more than posers. They love sitting around at tournaments drinking champagne and talking about how the game should be run.

>   BARRY HEARN.

After dealing with pop groups Alex is a saint.

>   HOWARD KRUGER.

We can get round Alex's tarnished image.

>   IBID.

I will chase him to the ends of the earth. I will never give up.

>   ALEX HIGGINS in pursuit of the £51,536 owed to him after the Kruger company managing him went into receivership.

A lot of people are getting hurt by people who, like this defendant [Kruger], are incompetent, reckless or worse. Kruger should have looked after his business but he certainly did not.

>   JUDGE DAVID JACKSON disqualifying Howard Kruger for five years from holding any company directorships.

The idea is to grind the opposition into the ground. That's on and off the table.

>   BARRY HEARN.

Aye, well, you can always *shoot* a dog.

>   GEORGE JACKSON, former manager of Patsy Fagan and others but now a full-time greyhound trainer.

19
Marriage

IF I had to make the choice between staying married and playing snooker, snooker would win.

> RAY REARDON.

WE weren't hoping for a boy or a girl, we were just happy to take pot luck.

> STEVE DAVIS.

WHEN people blamed my marriage for the state of my game I felt insulted as a professional sportsman.

> STEVE DAVIS.

20
Media

IF he sneezed, they'd say he spat on the floor.

>   BILL WERBENIUK on the press's treatment of Alex Higgins.

I used to be sober until I discovered snooker.

>   STEVE ACTESON, journalist.

THERE is a breed of newspapers and of reporters who work for them who are not interested in sport, human endeavour or even human interest. What they are here for is smut. They'll admit to it when privately cornered. They say it's what sells newspapers.

>   JANICE HALE, journalist.

AROUND the Table in 80 Days.
The Bill Werbeniuk Book of Aerobics.

>   IDEAS for books by journalists with time on their hands.

SOMETIMES I think I live in a holiday camp world where people say nice things to me all the time and the media wants to know what colour my underpants are.

>   STEVE DAVIS.

I miss that reading now. I think it's a great shame when so much space is given to violence.

> JOE DAVIS recalling a time when billiards was more widely and regularly reported.

By and large, but with some exceptions, sportsmen and the press have a love–hate relationship. We love them and they hate us.

> STEVE ACTESON.

21
Misbehaving

I'M on the front page for having a pee in a plant pot. Don't they realise the *Belgrano* has been sunk and that hundreds of lives have been lost?

>ALEX HIGGINS.

PERHAPS I should have head butted someone.

>STEVE DAVIS on the severity of his £12,000 fine for refusing to give a post-match interview.

WE were like a father and son. Alex always respected firmness. I had to slap him a few times to keep him in his place.

>DEL SIMMONS on managing Alex Higgins.

DEAN apologised and we told him he was a naughty boy.

>REX WILLIAMS on Dean Reynolds who was disciplined for remarks in a newspaper about players taking beta blockers.

I hope very much that the WPBSA will be sensible enough to take no action against Alex over this matter. Indeed, if there was any justice in the world, he ought to be awarded at least an OBE for his services to snooker instead of being knocked like this. Does anyone seriously think the game would be the attraction it is today without him?

>ANN WILTON, in a letter to *Snooker Scene*, on the alleged use of an expletive by Alex Higgins.

He had only three vices: drinking, gambling and women.

> JOHN MCLOUGHLIN, Alex Higgins' first manager.

This wasn't exactly *Pot Black*, was it?

> JUDGE CHRISTOPHER YOUNG to David Almey who admitted outraging public decency at a 'Gentlemen's Evening' at the Castle Snooker Club in Leicester.

Jon never did me nor the ref any harm – and come to think of it, he did not do any harm to the balls either.

> STEVE DAVIS on Jon Wright who potted only eight balls when losing 5–0 to Davis in the 1991 Rothmans Grand Prix. Wright seemed to have difficulty locating his chair after each visit to the table.

I want out of snooker. I want a normal life.

> JON WRIGHT.

22
Money

I am thinking of buying a couple of Monopoly games to try to learn what to do with it all.

> STEVE DAVIS.

THERE's too much money. All the fun's gone out of it. We're in the world of agents and managers now.

> RAY REARDON.

I'LL buy a forest if you buy a forest.

> STEVE DAVIS and Barry Hearn discussing buying a forest as a tax-avoidance device.

ONE day we'll be able to buy a bigger forest than the one Davis owns.

> IAN DOYLE.

GOD, £1000 for playing snooker. It was unbelievable to me.

> TERRY GRIFFITHS on the prize money he received as runner-up in the 1978 Pontins Open.

I don't find money exciting. I have always found it in the past quite an embarrassing subject to talk about. I always felt a little bit guilty that I earned money at what is effectively a game and a hobby.

> STEVE DAVIS.

I don't want to be a superstar. I want to earn superstar money.

JAMES WATTANA.

IF you do anything just for the money you don't succeed.

BARRY HEARN.

OVER the years that relationship with other players has changed – through the money, through the competitiveness, through the pressures of a weekly circuit we never used to have. Before, there were just one or two main tournaments a year. You could develop friendships when you were on tour or in exhibitions. Now there is a major championship every few weeks and with each you get the bitterness, the back-stabbing . . . they are all there now and I think it will get worse.

TERRY GRIFFITHS.

I did a job. I earned my wage and valued it. Many of today's players are big gamblers. They don't bet in tenners but in hundreds. They don't respect money because they never had to work hard for it.

RAY REARDON.

THE greatest feeling in the world is to put the biggest wad in your pocket. So big you can't get it out when you're sitting down.

KIRK STEVENS.

THE pursuit of glory can make a man invincible; the pursuit of money makes him vulnerable.

BARRY HEARN.

ANYBODY who says they can get bored playing for £100,000 at nineteen should think again. When I used to play for 50p at his age, I didn't get bored.

DENNIS TAYLOR on alleged remarks by Stephen Hendry that he was bored during his match with Taylor.

WHILE one wishes them well – like soccer players of the 1960s – snooker players are now in danger of becoming slaves to greed. The old players earned small money but did not have the same pressure. There was a lot more fun in the game, but I suppose in fairness, had the old players had the same opportunity to become tycoons they would have rushed to join the rat-race too.

TED LOWE.

EVEN if there wasn't any money in the game, I would still be down the snooker hall. Snooker is my life. I still enjoy going down the club with my mates for a few games, a few drinks and a few laughs.

JIMMY WHITE.

LESS than perfect financial circumstances are the keenest spur to further endeavour.

JOE DAVIS.

HE played pool for money and he loved money deeply and truly, loved even the dark engraving on the splendid paper of fresh bills. He could love the game of pool and the equipment of the game, the wood and cloth, the phenolic resin of the glossy balls, the finish of his phallic cue stick, the sounds and color of pool. But the thing he loved the most was money.

WALTER TEVIS, *The Color of Money*.

23
Nicknames

Hearn the Earn.
BARRY HEARN.

Steve 'Interesting' Davis.
NICKNAME created by the television programme *Spitting Image*.

The Golden Nugget.
STEVE DAVIS.

The Grinder.
CLIFF THORBURN.

The Methodical Mountie.
CLIFF THORBURN.

The Emperor of Pot.
JOE DAVIS.

The Wizard of Pot.
JOE DAVIS.

The King of the Cue.
JOE DAVIS.

The Mercurial Maestro of the Baize.

    JOE DAVIS.

The Sultan of Snooker.

    JOE DAVIS.

Potato Face.

    JOE DAVIS.

The Prince of Darkness.

    RAY REARDON.

Dracula.

    RAY REARDON.

Young Banger.

    REARDON's nickname as a child.

The Chief Inspector.

    RAY REARDON.

The Welsh Corgi.

    RAY REARDON.

The First Lady of Snooker.

    ALLISON FISHER.

The Whirlwind.

    JIMMY WHITE. (My mates call me The Wind actually.)

THE great W.T.
>WILLIE THORNE.

KING of Hearts.
>TONY KNOWLES.

THE Mighty Atom.
>W.J. PEALL, 5'1" billiard player.

THE Twickenham Terrier.
>MELBOURNE INMAN.

THE Red Ball King.
>GEORGE GRAY.

BALLCRUSHER.
>LEN GANLEY.

BILLY Thud.
>PERRIE MANS.

THE Clown Prince of Snooker.
>JACKIE REA.

STEADY Eddie.
>EDDIE CHARLTON.

THE Brother.
>FRED DAVIS.

Whispering Ted.

TED LOWE.

The Ginger Magician.

STEVE DAVIS.

Buzby.

NEAL FOULDS – because he's always on the phone.

Tornado.

TONY DRAGO.

Sniffer.

JOHN SPENCER.

The Man in the White Suit.

KIRK STEVENS.

Giro Jon.

JON WRIGHT – because of his habit of playing for money immediately after cashing his social security cheque.

Bionic Brat.

KIRK STEVENS – self-description.

Hurricane.

ALEX HIGGINS. (I wanted to be billed as Alexander the Great. Anyway he wasn't as fast as me. Now I'm Hurricane Higgins.)

IRVING 'the Deacon' Crane.

> US pool player.

JOE 'the Meatman' Balsis.

> US pool player.

LOU 'Machine-gun' Butera.

> US pool player.

24
Oddballs

BECAUSE Steve was quiet and school work came fairly easy to him, I pictured him in a branch of local government.

JEAN DAVIS, Steve's mum.

BUT you've got to remember there's always three sides to every story – Alex's version, the other person's version . . . and the truth.

HOWARD KRUGER.

IT's a game to be played in clogs and corduroys or by navvies in their lunch hours.

TOM REECE, billiards artist, on snooker.

TOMATO game.

IBID.

THERE is life beyond Skegness.

GRAHAM CRIPSEY.

ON the eighth day God created Alex Higgins.

LEGEND on T-shirt worn by fan during the 1983 World Championship.

I am writing to ask why every time Alex Higgins makes a foul he wants the rules changing.

LETTER to *Snooker Scene* from D. Wigglesworth.

It is a lucky, flukey game and I don't want to know about it.

>   WALTER LINDRUM'S response to Joe Davis's idea that he take up snooker.

Let's see some heavy legend action here.

>   TOM CRUISE to Paul Newman in the film *The Color of Money*.

Whoever called snooker 'chess with balls' was rude but right.

>   CLIVE JAMES.

Steve may be a man and a champion to millions, but at home he's still our boy and if he sits in my chair I'll tell him and he gets out quickly.

>   BILL DAVIS, Steve's father.

I never wear underpants.

>   BILL WERBENIUK revealing a secret he managed to keep hidden when his trousers split during his televised match with David Taylor during the 1980 World Cup.

I thought Bill had it sewn up.

>   CLIFF THORBURN, Canadian captain, on the above event.

We're not into minority sports.

>   BARRY HEARN denying rumours that he was going to bid for Manchester United.

The suggestion will receive consideration at an early date but it seems a little doubtful whether snooker as a spectacular game is sufficiently popular to warrant the successful promotion of such a competition.

>   A. STANLEY THORN, then secretary of the BA&CC, responding in 1923 to a suggestion that the organisation introduce a professional championship.

'SNOOKER Loopy'.

> TITLE of song recorded by Chas 'n' Dave with backing vocals from Matchroom players Steve Davis, Dennis Taylor, Terry Griffiths, Tony Meo and Willie Thorne.

'THE Wanderer'.

> TITLE of song recorded by 'Four Away' consisting of Alex Higgins, Jimmy White, Tony Knowles and Kirk Stevens.

IT gives the old something to talk to the young about.

> CHINESE official on snooker which was banned during the Cultural Revolution but is now making a comeback.

WE hold 'pageant of the horse' for the horsey set so why shouldn't we do something for the working class who cannot afford a horse?

> COUNCILLOR JACK BROWN defending South Yorkshire County Council's decision to organise a snooker and pool competition as part of 'working-class culture'. Other activities to be included were whippet and greyhound racing.

THERE'S an innocence and enthusiasm about him that could make him the newest recruit in the seminary.

> ANGELA LEVIN, journalist, on Steve Davis.

YOU can tell when Kirk is thinking. When he is not thinking he looks like an Easter Island statue with a sinus problem. When he is thinking, he still looks like that, but licks his lips.

> CLIVE JAMES on Kirk Stevens.

KIRK Stevens has done for snooker what Persil did for washing, what Kermit did for frogs and what Tarzan did for the jungle. In other words he has layered the game with pink and white marzipan, made it nice, touched it with the Sound of Music and Mary Poppins and left it bubbling with show-biz home-cooked schmaltz.

> TED CORBETT, journalist.

WE used to be the sport of tobacco and booze, but now we are rubbing shoulders with investment companies and the like.

BARRY HEARN.

ALEX is remarkable, you know. If Alex went to a psychiatrist, the psychiatrist would have to see a psychiatrist.

RONNIE HARPER, journalist, on Alex Higgins.

YOU look like Mickey Mouse with a welding shield on.

EDDIE CHARLTON on Dennis Taylor's Joe 90 glasses.

I love the snooker world, the male aggressive thing of it.

BARRY HEARN.

WHEN the world is wrong, hardly to be endured, I shall return to Thurston's Hall and there smoke a pipe among the connoisseurs of top and side. It is as near to the Isle of Innisfree as we can get within a hundred leagues of Leicester Square.

J.B. PRIESTLY paying homage to Thurston's, a name synonymous with billiards and snooker for more than 150 years. The premises were destroyed by German bombing during the Second World War.

THE only way I could afford to eat here would be to do it through a building society.

NORMAN DAGLEY'S reaction to studying the menu at the Hilton Hotel in Malta during the 1971 World Amateur Billiards Championship.

WE know Higgins is a bit of a case but he's a great snooker player – perhaps as good as any the world has seen. Normal human beings would drop down dead if they tried to live like Higgins – if they stretched themselves to that degree. Yet if he tried to change at all, if he stopped to think, he'd no longer be Higgins. The beauty of Higgins is that he's magnificently ignorant. He doesn't know what the hell he's doing – yet when he goes to that snooker table he makes magic happen.

DENNIS TAYLOR in an interview with Terry Broadhurst in the *Burnley Evening Star*.

IT used to be so important to me to have the approval of the older players. Then I realised that they would never give it to me.

KIRK STEVENS.

HE is a great player. He should be in the top sixteen. We come from the same planet.

STEVE DAVIS on Alain Robidoux whom he narrowly beat 5–4 in the 1988 Fidelity International.

I'VE just met a snooker player on the train with the most beautiful manners. His name was Higgins. Have you heard of him?

MOTHER-IN-LAW of the editor of the *Observer*, Donald Trelford.

THE game has lost its sleaze and it's all the poorer for that. Snooker was exciting when it was raw and new and the halls were a haven for boys skipping school. Jimmy White was sixteen and lived in a council house in Tooting with a broken door bell. Now he's as respectable as a bishop.

JULIE WELCH, journalist.

ACTUALLY, did you know that Steve's not a real person at all? He's a robot. Take his trousers down and you'll see 'Made in Hong Kong' stamped on his bum.

BARRY HEARN on Steve Davis.

Cut off that goddam sunshine.

> MINNESOTA FATS in the novel *The Hustler* to a janitor who had opened the curtains at nine o'clock in the morning in a pool room where he and Fast Eddie Felson had played all night.

Forget night life. It's all about snooker.

> JAMES WATTANA.

Why snooker is still an obsession I'm not too sure. If you look at it one way, I've got nothing else to do.

> STEVE DAVIS.

What would be brilliant for the sport would be to find a player with all the natural flair and flamboyance of Higgins – but without the aggro.

> IBID.

There are 2000 players in London as good as Hendry.

> RON CLOVER, then manager of Stephen Hendry, to Ian Doyle during negotiations to buy Hendry's contract.

Some game this is if there's 2000 in London as good as him.

> IAN DOYLE's reply.

Letting your children watch Wimbledon unsupervised would be like leaving them alone with a video nasty. Yet from watching snooker they can only profit

THE fellow feeling among snooker players [is] like the fellow feeling among musicians; they all labour long and hard before finding out whether they are anything special, and if it turns out that they are, they give credit to the fates and not to themselves. Tributes to another's craft are common. There are some powerfully developed egos at championship level, but that essential modesty always shows through the conceit. Davis, in addition to a strategic brain ranking with Reardon's, has the physical and/or mental ability not to miss the easy one at the critical moment. For as long as he retains that capacity, he will win more often than not. To the superficial eye this makes him a bit dull, like Bjorn Borg or Billie-Jean King. But really the self-discipline of those great champions when they were ahead was the most exciting thing tennis had to offer. Letting your children watch Wimbledon unsupervised would be like leaving them alone with a video nasty. Yet from watching snooker they can only profit. Snooker has no room for a Nastase or a McEnroe. A snooker match lasts too long, makes too many demands on inner resources, not just of the will but of the spirit. It is more like a war than a battle. It is more like life.

CLIVE JAMES.

THE world of snooker was rocked to its foundations last night when the crowded auditorium of the Sheffield Crucible witnessed amazing scenes involving snooker's bad boy Mr Alex 'Hurricocaine' Higgins. Halfway through the first frame, spectators and TV viewers gasped as the veteran Northern Ireland ace and former world champion bent down over the table and deliberately hit a ball. Said one close observer, 'I couldn't believe my eyes. Alex had been behaving quite normally up until then, missing everything and uttering obscenities, when suddenly and without provocation he bashed this poor red ball right into a pocket.' Officials last night refused to comment on Higgins's outrageous behaviour. Said a spokesman for BOWTIE [Snooker's governing body] 'We will have to see a video replay of the alleged incident before doing nothing. Mr Higgins knows the score. It's 10–0.' However last night Higgins was unrepentant. 'I know what I am. People pay to see me smacking the balls about a bit. They would soon get bored if all I did was to go round head-butting officials and issuing death threats to my opponents.' Ted Lowe is 108.

PRIVATE EYE

25
Playing

My feeling for the game is raw. Never mind the coaching manuals – I hit the balls while I'm still on the hoof. I go for the 'impossible' pots no one else would consider. Pure, basic, instinctive snooker; the hunter hunting and the crowd baying for more.

    ALEX HIGGINS.

The pockets look like mouse's ears and the balls look as though they've got to travel half a mile to get there.

    JOHN VIRGO after his defeat by Stephen Murphy in the 1991 Pearl Assurance British Open.

All the pleasure comes either in anticipation or retrospect. On the table, everything is mortified groping.

    MARTIN AMIS, novelist and serious part-time player.

The only side he hasn't attempted is suicide.

    RAY REARDON on Alex Higgins.

It takes a couple of years to learn how to sit out – that is to wait your turn – and then whatever the other man's done – to play your best game right away.

    JOE DAVIS.

To control the cue ball you must be in control of the cue and to control the cue you must be in control of yourself.

    FRANK CALLAN, snooker coach.

HAVE you ever heard of Frank Sinatra?
Yes.
Well then. Treat them like Frank Sinatra.

>CONVERSATION between BARRY HEARN and a Thai snooker organiser who was unsure how to treat snooker players.

THESE snooker players have it good. When they play a bad shot the crowd don't shout 'Get off, you bum.' They haven't got another ten men bolstering their confidence or ruining it.

>KEVIN MORAN, Republic of Ireland international footballer.

STEVE Davis and Stephen Hendry play a different type of game. Davis strangles you slowly, while Hendry knocks you flat.

>TERRY GRIFFITHS.

THE last frame is the hardest to win.

>STEPHEN HENDRY.

WHEN a one-legged snooker player from Iceland is drawn against a man who won the world championship three times, there can only be one result. Brynjar Valdimarsson beat John Spencer, 5-1.

>DAVID HUNN, journalist.

I am looking forward to interpreting the intensity of excitement at the magic moment of stillness between shots.

>ROY FREER, artist, on his plan to paint the contestants in the final of the 1988 Fidelity International.

HE came in with a jar of speed pills to stay awake. But I really knew he had come to play when he laid out three pairs of socks.

>CLIFF THORBURN recalling playing for fifty-four hours against Canadian Dick in San Francisco.

It's like pressing an invisible button inside you. You just go into overdrive. It's unbelievable, the silkiest feeling in the world. You feel like a prima ballerina. You've got touch, sensitivity and power. It's better because you've sat and suffered, waiting for the moment.

>   ALEX HIGGINS.

Stephen is absolute perfection – I can die happy now.

>   FRANK CALLAN on Stephen Hendry.

I know that such a shot is full of risks, but it is full of poetry, the charming poetry of motion. And, to my mind, playing it or leaving it alone marks the distinction between a workman and an artist.

>   JOHN ROBERTS JNR discussing a difficult shot.

Potting is memory.

>   JOHN SPENCER.

This must be an easy game, I thought, and I took to it right away.

>   STEPHEN HENDRY'S reaction to playing on a quarter-size table he received as a Christmas present. Within two weeks he had made a break of 50.

When I'm really playing well, I don't know who I'm playing.

>   STEVE DAVIS.

You get nothing for rushing.

>   FRANK CALLAN.

If your thought processes have jagged edges this will show itself in your shot.

>   IBID.

NOT for Reardon, Charlton, Davis, Mans *et al.* kisses to the crowd after potting a black, or histrionic gesticulation when missing one. There is only professionalism and a desire to get on with the game in the right spirit. I'd say snooker is a better character builder than many another sport.

JOHN BURROWS, journalist.

LOVE the game and the game will love you.

CLIVE EVERTON.

IT has often been said that people would pay to watch Alex Higgins drink a half of lager.

JANICE HALE, journalist.

WHAT I want to see in Steve's eyes is something suggesting anaesthesia. If they look dead, that's good. It means he's into it.

BARRY HEARN on Steve Davis.

I love playing snooker, but it's so hard. It's harder than the wall of death.

GRAHAM CRIPSEY, a former wall of death rider.

THAT'S the idea of safety play – to leave your opponent dead on the baulk cushion.

CLIVE EVERTON.

I was very careful and I felt hard and mean. I don't think I can play much better than that. I had a good day. I was in wonderland.

CLIFF THORBURN after beating Stephen Hendry 9–1 in the semi-final of the 1987 Fidelity International.

PLAYING Bill is like playing for pints of blood.

CLIFF THORBURN on Bill Werbeniuk.

Playing snooker gives you firm hands and helps to build up character. It is the ideal recreation for dedicated nuns

I haven't played as well as that since London Bridge was a lighthouse.

>   PAT HOULIHAN after beating Chris Ross 9–1 in the 1978 World Championship.

THERE are two old Belgians who will back themselves for a thousand francs that they can get so much side on the ball that they can make smoke rise from the cloth.

>   RICHARD HELMSTETTER, cue maker.

WE like the click of the balls and the coordination of the game. Also nuns always have an eye for colour. Because we are dressed in black and white, the red, yellow, green, brown, blue and pink of the balls appeal to us.

>   MOTHER JOHN BAPTIST of the Benedictine Order of the Adorers of the Sacred Heart of Jesus of Montmartre who pray for the 100 martyrs of the Reformation on snooker during a competition among the nuns to raise money for the restoration of Tyburn Convent in London.

PLAYING snooker gives you firm hands and helps to build up character. It is the ideal recreation for dedicated nuns.

>   ARCHBISHOP BARBARITO, the Pope's emissary to Britain, on the above competition.

JIMMY WHITE has the nervous system of a fighter pilot on amphetamines.

>   CLIVE JAMES.

RAYMOND Priestley of Melbourne tried the snooker shot of a lifetime – suspended upside down over the table, hanging by his legs from the rafters. But he slipped, crashed head first on the concrete floor and died.

>   REPORT in the *Daily Telegraph*.

A ball is a ball and they each have to be potted.

>   JOE DAVIS.

In snooker possession is ten parts of the law. While one man is at the table and scoring, his opponent is as impotent as a eunuch.

HUGH MCILVANNEY, journalist.

If I'm 90 in front I'll still snooker a guy. You've got to kill.

STEVE DAVIS.

I want everyone to know that they don't enjoy playing me, which is one of the reasons why I don't talk too much until after the game is over.

CLIFF THORBURN.

Once you lose the happiness in your game you start to think wrong.

STEVE DAVIS.

If you murder a player, he'll be psychologically beaten before he gets on the table next time.

STEPHEN HENDRY.

The Breaks Came My Way.

JOE DAVIS, title of memoirs.

The game still fascinates me as a problem, and I am always studying my own play and that of others and testing theories.

IBID.

The more you can think subconsciously in a special kind of 'snooker language' if you like, the better your concentration is likely to be.

REX WILLIAMS.

AT snooker or billiards you will never attain any kind of rhythm if you spend ten seconds over one shot, two minutes over the next, half a minute over the next and so on. If you can manage to play at a steady regular pace your game will tend to blend harmoniously together instead of looking like a series of isolated shots.

>   IBID.

Do your thinking beforehand and not during a shot.

>   IBID.

DON'T play as if life depended on winning, for that creates tension, which is fatal to timing.

>   FRED DAVIS.

THE pleasure of potting a ball is almost sensual.

>   BRENDA FRICKER, Oscar-winning actress.

No gentleman should be capable of making a break of more than 25.

>   KING EDWARD VII.

WHAT I like about it is that when you're on, nobody can interfere. The table's yours.

>   JOHN ALDERTON, actor.

POT Black? I'm having a struggle to pot anything.

>   JOHN PULMAN.

I might damage the cloth.

>   THE PRINCESS ROYAL, then Princess Anne, declining to play when opening Harrows' Leisure Centre.

I'VE always enjoyed playing but I've never cared much for a lot of the things that go with it.

    FRED DAVIS.

WHEN that last ball went down I felt a lump in my throat.

    ANONYMOUS PLAYER during the 1982 Embassy World Championship.

> A young lad from Belfast came to our town last year
> They all came to see him from far and near
> He broke off with nineties, he knocked up the ton
> There's no better player the other side of Brum
> The crowds were all laughing and suffering from shock
> Norman Vaughan wasn't there but he still beat the clock
> His four minute break of 104
> Just proved to the visitors how fast he could score
> He gets up too quick when he plays at the ball
> But the amazing thing is, it still manages to fall
> He's superb with the rest, his action is great
> And his positional play shows he's just got the weight.
> He can screw a ball maybe three feet or two
> But I'm sure if he tried he could screw it to Crewe.
> He's played with a patch over one of his eyes
> Chalked up ninety-seven and I'm telling no lies.
> Now my dear reader if you haven't already guessed
> The name of this chap is not Georgie Best
> His name's Alex Higgins, he's always on form
> Just go and see him and watch him perform.

    'THE CHAMP' by David Guildford.

EVERYBODY who plays Steve these days seems to play as if he's hypnotised.

    RAY EDMONDS after losing 9–0 to Steve Davis in the semi-final of the 1981 John Courage English Professional Championship.

IT'S a simple game, son. Just treat them like eggs.

    GEORDIE KIRKWOOD, a friend of Alex Higgins.

IF I can play like this, practising and without eating, I must be the best in the world.

> ALEX HIGGINS, who during the 1982 World Championship decided to eat only vitamin pills because the hotel food was not to his liking. It must have worked because he won the championship.

THE game is an art and many of its severest tests of skill are called for before a ball is struck. This is a fundamental fact – to understand it is to be given a valuable key; to acquire good technique is to open the door to all the pleasure and riches the game can offer.

> JACK KARNEHM.

SNOOKER is an intellectual game really. It's like chess. The only difference is you play it with balls.

> TONY MEO.

TOUCH is the sweetness of your delivery and the perfection of your timing.

> JACK KARNEHM.

THE application of stun and screw are the 'Shots of the Game'.

> EDDIE CHARLTON.

THE whole idea of the game is to make your opponent feel miserable, keeping him sitting out, shut out, excluded.

> CLIVE EVERTON.

I started to study break-building, positional play, safety play and the general strategy of the game, and became so interested that whenever something happened which surprised me, I immediately made a mental note, and afterwards went away by myself and tried the thing out to see what happened and why.

> JOE DAVIS.

EVEN today, after I have retired from world's championship play, I am still learning and still adjusting my ideas, for I still come across shots in this game of infinite variety which elude me, and as soon as possible afterwards I experiment until I thoroughly understand why the shot has beaten me, and how to overcome the problem. It is through this intense study that I have held my own as the world's number one snooker player for so long. But I will go further than that and assert I have never ceased to improve my snooker, and that in fact I am a better player this year than I was last, and that there has never been a time since I first started to play snooker that I have not been able to say the same thing.

IBID.

SOMETIMES I feel like a boxer. I get a bloke down and I don't mind hurting him. In fact, I get great pleasure doing it. We are both in the ring and we know the rules.

STEPHEN HENDRY.

IT was like the Colosseum in Rome. They wanted his head and I wanted to give it to them.

EUGENE HUGHES after losing 5–4 to Steve Davis in the 1985 Benson & Hedges Irish Masters.

PLAY the balls, not your opponent.

SNOOKER saying.

AND then Fats began moving around the table, making balls, all his former ponderousness gone now, his motions like ballet, the steps light, sure and rehearsed; the bridge hand inevitably falling into the right place; the hand on the butt of the cue with its fat jeweled fingers gently pushing the thin shaft into the cue ball. He never stopped to look at the layout of the balls, never appeared to think or to prepare himself for shooting. About every five shots he stopped long enough to stroke the tip of his cue gently with chalk; but he did not even look at the table as he did this; he merely watched what he was doing at the moment.

FROM *The Hustler* by Walter Tevis.

THEN Eddie started winning. He felt it start in the middle of a game, began to feel the sense he sometimes had of being part of the table and of the balls and of the cue stick.

> IBID.

IN the event of the yellow ball being involved in a foul stroke it is the custom for the watchers to cry out the word 'bollocks'.

> ONE of the rules of Savile Snooker.

I felt my hand touch a red so I had no option but to call a foul. I'm desperate to win but I'm not that desperate.

> TERRY GRIFFITHS.

I like my players to be fit but it's hard with someone like Jimmy White who trains on vodka and night clubs.

> BARRY HEARN.

THESE cushions are at least stopping the balls falling on the floor.

> JOHN PULMAN.

ALL roads lead to the black.

> JOE DAVIS.

IN Australia I'm considered an attacking player.

> EDDIE CHARLTON.

THE match was very scrappy for the first two sessions. I was very nervous for the first one and so relaxed for the second that I asked someone what was the opposite of a beta blocker because I needed to get my heart going a bit.

> TERRY GRIFFITHS.

THAT miss on the red will go straight out of my head as soon as I collect my pension book.

>JOHN PARROTT on a crucial red missed when playing Steve Davis in the final of the 1988 Mercantile Credit Classic.

IT's nice to be an all-rounder and to be able to change your style. In the first half it was necessary to be patient, in the second half it was necessary to flow.

>STEVE DAVIS.

THE recession only became apparent for us round about Christmas. It seems that the lads' night out is the last thing to go. First they cut down on clothes, wives, children etc. then finally they decide they can't afford to play snooker three nights a week, only two.

>STEPHEN DENNISON of Riley Snooker Clubs.

THE British Board of Censors will not pass any seduction scene unless the seducer has one foot on the floor. Apparently, sex in England is something like snooker.

>FRED ALLEN, American humorist.

ALEX Higgins is the nearest snooker equivalent to the gun-fighters from the Old West who stroll through the swing doors of the saloon ready to test their claim to be quicker on the draw than any local hero.

>CLIVE EVERTON.

26
Pool

DRESSING a pool player in a tuxedo is like putting whipped cream on a hot dog.

>   MINNESOTA FATS.

BUMS play pool, gentlemen play billiards.

>   DANNY MCGOORTY, billiard player.

EVERY player's an egotist. You get four drinks in a guy and he's never lost a game. You get ten in him and he's never missed a shot.

>   DON WILLIS, pool player.

GREATER love hath no man than to lay down his life behind the eight ball.

>   LUTHER LASSITER.

I didn't sign a contract that says I shoot pool for life. (Fast Eddie) It's been signed for you. (Minnesota Fats)

>   CONVERSATION between Fast Eddie Felson and Minnesota Fats in *The Color of Money* by Walter Tevis.

PEOPLE won't pay to watch pool games. We're not rock singers.

>   MINNESOTA FATS.

HE had been shy when he was twelve and thirteen, before he first picked up a pool stick. When he found out about pool and how well he could play it, it changed him. He could not remember all of it, but it had even changed the way he walked.

FROM *THE COLOR OF MONEY* by Walter Tevis.

To stroke and hit the cue ball, to watch the colored ball roll with the certitude that he himself imposed on it, to see and hear the colored ball fall into the pocket he had chosen, was exquisite.

IBID.

A pool hustler had to do what he claimed to be able to do. The risks he took were not underwritten. His skill on the arena of green cloth – cloth that was itself the color of money – could never be only pretense. Pool players were often cheats and liars, petty men whose lives were filled with pretensions, who ran out on their women and walked away from their debts; but on the table, with the lights overhead beneath the cigarette smoke and the silent crowd around them in whatever dive of a billiard parlor at four in the morning, they had to find the wherewithal inside themselves to do more than promise excellence. Under whatever lies might fill the life, the excellence had to be there. It had to be delivered. It could not be faked.

IBID.

PEOPLE thought pool hustling was corrupt and sleazy, worse than boxing. But to win at pool, to be a professional at it, you had to deliver. In a business you could pretend that skill and determination had brought you along when it had only been luck and muddle; a pool hustler did not have the freedom to believe that.

IBID.

27
The Powers That Be

THEY are a self-appointed governing body from the backwoods of Bristol. They have a parochial approach.

>BARRY HEARN on the WPBSA. He later joined the board.

MONEY has been squandered on people and things that don't matter. They spend all their time thinking of ways of getting at Barry Hearn or trying to frighten people by threatening disciplinary action.

>FRED DAVIS on the WPBSA.

THE man should quit snooker and go off to Disneyland. He'd be a bigger attraction than Mickey Mouse because nothing he says can be taken seriously.

>IAN DOYLE on Rex Williams.

I am deeply upset that after all my efforts for the players, I did not receive one letter from a fellow professional thanking me for all my work over the years. There were letters from other professional people and my friends but not one from a player. That hurt.

>REX WILLIAMS resigning from the board of the WPBSA.

I was on the board myself for a short time at the start of the 1980s and I know that players are no good at anything but playing snooker. They should stick to it. In the old days when there was precious little money coming into the game, we didn't have much to worry about. But now snooker has grown so much and there are many difficult decisions to make and I am worried about the game being sold short, and players are not the best people to make these decisions. Players are emotional people who are naturally affected by their own form; that is what they worry about most. Businessmen work only on percentages. A snooker player's first duty is to himself and although they could advise a professional board of businessmen about playing conditions, that is all they know. If players have time to devote to politics – and I haven't – there must be something wrong.

STEVE DAVIS.

28
Practice

CONSTANT practice is very hard but I get great joy out of it when it goes right.

STEVE DAVIS.

YOU practise to find out how your body works. I know every aspect of my technical game so well, I can fine tune it. You practise certain things that make you strong. I get better, quicker now.

STEVE DAVIS.

I'VE never been one to spend all my time practising. My attitude being what it is, I'd go mad. I've never practised more than an hour at a time and I like to be alone.

FRED DAVIS.

WHEN I was younger I'd buy a couple of drinks and rolls and make myself reach a 50 break to get a drink and 100 to get a bite of a roll. That was a good way to starve. Maybe that's why I'm so slim.

STEVE DAVIS.

I'M probably at my happiest when I've been playing badly. And then I get down on the practice table and it all starts to come back – like a revelation. And that is something that is forever going on, you're forever going out of tune. And every time you do it it's 'Ah, bloody hell, I've been standing a bit wrong.' And it all falls into place and I think, 'Cor, I'm looking forward to the next tournament.'

STEVE DAVIS.

NEVER be self-satisfied, always spur yourself on and keep practising.

JOE DAVIS.

IF the four-minute warning went off sounding the end of the world, Steve would take time to practise snooker.

BARRY HEARN on Steve Davis.

I'M an easy player to beat. I can't practise hours a day on safety, hours with the rest, hours with the spider. It drives me crazy. But I suppose I'm going to have to do all those things – one day.

WILLIE THORNE.

IT'S beneficial, it's therapeutic and I love doing it. Because my enjoyment is not necessarily in the winning, but in the doing of it.

STEVE DAVIS.

WHEN I am out of touch at snooker, I practise billiards again to get back all the strokes which you need constantly in billiards but only occasionally in snooker.

JOE DAVIS.

I don't have a problem with monotony.

STEVE DAVIS on the need for constant practice.

I am going back to Canada to practise, practise and practise until I want to eat my cue.

JIM WYCH after going out of the 1987 Embassy World Championship.

THERE'S so much to learn.

STEVE DAVIS'S reply when asked why he practised so much.

29
Pressure

I<small>F</small> you can play as if it means nothing when it means everything, you've got it.

> S<small>TEVE</small> D<small>AVIS</small> on how to cope with pressure.

I<small>NCURABLY</small> aware of his presence, cool and distant, they have the look of sailors who can hear the creak of the iceberg.

> H<small>UGH</small> M<small>CILVANNEY</small>, journalist, on Steve Davis's fellow professionals.

I've gone through periods when I honestly didn't want someone to leave me the last red and all the colours. The game takes over your life. The game's a killer. If you get a losing streak it snowballs out of all proportion. I wish I could enjoy the pressure all the time. Sometimes I do, sometimes I don't.

> J<small>OHN</small> V<small>IRGO</small>.

H<small>AS</small> anybody got a rope?

> M<small>IKE</small> H<small>ALLETT</small> as he let a lead of 7–0 and 8–2 slip against Stephen Hendry in the Benson & Hedges final in 1991.

I cracked out there once or twice. I've cracked a zillion times. No player can say he's never cracked. The difference about a great player is that he can go like that and then pull himself together and come on strong again. I know that's something I can do. When you feel the change come through your cue arm you have to try to relax and get back into a grooved rhythm just as golfers do. You have to summon up the muscle memory.

> S<small>TEVE</small> D<small>AVIS</small>.

Scar tissue forms on boxers' eyebrows but in snooker players' minds.

CLIVE EVERTON.

If there's enough pressure you can miss anything.

CLIFF THORBURN.

His talent is so frighteningly substantial that it tends to pervade the table even when he is seated, quiet and ostensibly hostile, a dozen feet away.

HUGH MCILVANNEY on Steve Davis.

Anybody who is embarrassed about showing anxiety will never be great. If your ego is so fragile that you can imagine you are invincible you won't make it.

STEVE DAVIS.

The more pressure I feel, the better I play. I don't have to worry about my image. I just have to beat Steve Davis.

STEPHEN HENDRY.

In snooker, that pressure is like the force of gravity bearing down on the players' heads.

ANGELA PATMORE, journalist.

The trouble with snooker is that the pressure tends to build up inside your head.

CLIFF THORBURN.

When you're in a match your very soul is out there for everybody to see. It's a kind of nightmare.

STEVE DAVIS.

I sometimes think there's no interim state between complacency and panic.

> BARRY HEARN.

I used to go to bed and I'd think, Jesus, what are you doing? But I'd have to get up the next day and do it all again and again and that went on for months. I felt the people were like woodpeckers pecking away at me all the time.

> TERRY GRIFFITHS on the pressures of being a top snooker player.

I think I'm just trying too darned hard. I'm probably trying to please a lot of people I don't even know, just trying to overcome a lot of bad publicity and a lot of negative emphasis.

> KIRK STEVENS on losing form.

IT's a lonely spot to be in. You can't cry the blues because you get so much benefit out of it when things go well. But there must be a hundred thousand guys out there saying: I wish I could play that guy. And that's how you feel.

> KIRK STEVENS.

I'M in the swamp now.

> KIRK STEVENS lamenting having to play in the qualifying stage of the Embassy World Championship.

OBVIOUSLY these guys have never played snooker at Thunder Bay in North Ontario when your bet is the last five bucks you have in the world. If you don't win you don't eat and it's sometimes 30 below outside. Believe me when it's as heavy as that you learn to play your safety shots before you even learn to sink a red.

> CLIFF THORBURN responding to claims that his style of play is boring.

PRESSURE is only pressure if you can't control it.

> JOHN PARROTT.

I'm in the swamp now

I'M a Buddhist. I don't worry about what happens next.

JAMES WATTANA.

THEY talk about pressure but I think pressure comes with lack of confidence. Everybody suffers from pressure but if you've got the confidence you overcome it. When you lose that bit of confidence the pressure really comes on because you start thinking about missing shots. When you're in full flow, you don't think about missing.

JOHN SPENCER.

ADRENALIN is my buzz and I love pressure.

PETER EBDON.

SNOOKER is the toughest game there is. It sends them all batty in the end.

ROBBO BRAZIER, Steve Davis's minder.

I used to laugh when people talked about pressure, but now I know what it means. It's all right on the way up and I suppose it's all right once you're there, but it's when you're almost there but not quite you seem to get the worst of it.

JOHN VIRGO.

THE difference between success and failure at the top level is less often one of technique than the ability to apply or withstand various types of pressure.

CLIVE EVERTON.

IT was then I thought about suicide. My whole world had come crashing in. Everywhere I turned there were creditors waiting for me. I felt like ending it all but didn't have the guts.

WILLIE THORNE.

I have never seen anyone more intense than Steve was that day. He was scary even to be sitting ten feet away from. He had eyes like a shark. I felt like Little Bo Peep surrounded by wolves.

KIRK STEVENS on Steve Davis after their clash in the 1984 Coral UK Open.

ALL my life as a working man I switched jobs to earn enough money for my family. That is what I call real pressure. By comparison playing snooker is money for old rope.

TERRY GRIFFITHS.

I was looking down my cue and all I could see was nightmares.

KIRK STEVENS after his 10–4 defeat by Steve Longworth in the 1987 Embassy World Championship.

30
Referees

THE sign of a good referee is when he's heard and not seen.

    IAN WILLIAMSON.

I'VE got the badge. If a player gives me problems he gets one warning. After that he's disqualified.

    DARREN SHAW, thirteen, believed to be the youngest referee to take charge of a match involving a professional player.

YOU have to play the break with the player all the time, know which ball he's going to play, and five or six after that. You have to flow with him, be with his mood, not be slow putting a ball back. You must keep up his momentum for him.

    LEN GANLEY.

THE ideal referee makes no remarks, calls the score regularly, is always ready with the rest and stands well away in the shadows with an ever-watchful eye. He also knows the rules.

    FRED DAVIS.

TOO many of them have gathered their knowledge from books. None of them can play.

    ALEX HIGGINS.

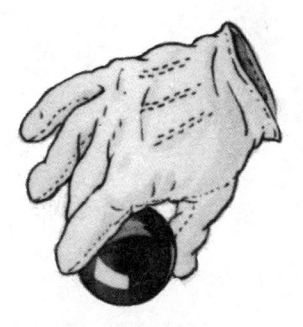

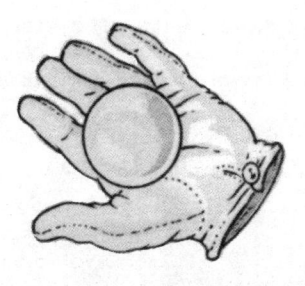

The sign of a good referee is when he's heard and not seen

Chorus:
Everybody's doing the Len Ganley stance,
Everybody's doing the Len Ganley stance. *(Repeat)*

Keep your arms as rigid as a juggernaut,
Clench your fist, point your knuckles straight ahead,
Do your best to look like a teddy bear,
Then try and pretend to look vertically dead.

Chorus:

Praise the lord, you all look so beautiful,
Bulging waistcoats, thirty inch at neck,
Shine your shoes and head for the Crucible,
Brush the baize and keep the crowd in check.

FROM the album 'Back in the DHSS' by Half Man Half Biscuit, 1986.

31
Retirement

OBSESSIONS don't fall apart overnight.

> STEVE DAVIS dismissing talk of his retirement.

It's been so long since I've been on TV people think I've retired.

> CLIFF THORBURN.

WELL chaps, I would like to announce my retirement – the events of the past few weeks have been unbearable. I don't want ever in my lifetime to have anything less than job satisfaction. Steve James, he's a nice lad, but I am not playing again. You can shove snooker up your jacksey. This game is the most corrupt in the world and it needs to be brought to the Department of Trade and Industry. I don't want to be part of it any more. I have had all sorts of shit thrown at me by the media in the past six or seven years. I have taken the brunt. I'm absolutely sick. It has interrupted my private life, my children's life and a few relationships. Let's see how you do without me, because I ain't playing no more. I might do a few overseas trips and teach kids. I don't like the WPBSA – the way they do things. They can throw me out, shove me out. I couldn't give a damn.

> ALEX HIGGINS announcing his retirement after being knocked out of the 1987 World Championships. He later changed his decision.

32
Self-image

I'M a bit of a loner but I'm not lonely.

    STEVE DAVIS.

NOBODY's as fast as me, nobody's as attractive as me to watch. I'm the best player who ever played the game.

    ALEX HIGGINS.

I have always been confident in my own ability, although equally I have always had a great deal of respect for my opponent's ability as well.

    TERRY GRIFFITHS.

I'M a snooker player, not an achiever.

    STEVE DAVIS.

I know I'm the best in the world – I've just got to prove it.

    WILLIE THORNE.

'THE People's Champion'.

    ALEX HIGGINS.

I had a personality by-pass when I was about seventeen.

    STEVE DAVIS.

WHEN I came into the world they threw the blueprint away.

ALEX HIGGINS.

A bit handy.

JIMMY WHITE on his abilities.

I was always a bit sharp. At school I had kids washing cars, window cleaning and gardening. I fixed up the jobs, they did them and I took 25 per cent.

BARRY HEARN.

I'VE tried being flash. But I'm afraid I'm not very good at it.

STEVE DAVIS.

I think it's fair to say that with a bit of luck I could have won the [World] Championship three times. But I also have to say that the reason I haven't won it is because I wasn't good enough. If I had been I wouldn't have needed the luck.

EDDIE CHARLTON.

I merely commercialised snooker.

JOE DAVIS.

I'M not quick enough to challenge Desert Orchid but I'm quicker around the bend.

ALEX HIGGINS.

THERE'S a snooker player inside me. I just have to open the zipper and let him out.

JIM WYCH after losing 5–2 to Dennis Taylor in the 1988 Fidelity International.

I guess I'm just a funniosity.

    FRED DAVIS.

I'M not a library player. But I don't go rushing round the table leaving my shoes behind either.

    JOHN PARROTT.

WHAT is amazing is that the whole of England is like one big holiday camp for me. You know what it's like when you're a kid and you're in the camp and everyone's being nice to you. It's all 'Hello, can I do anything for you?' Well that's a bit like my life.

    STEVE DAVIS.

I'M Thai. I'm different. I can be anything I want.

    JAMES WATTANA.

I'M a right bastard when I'm playing.

    JOHN PULMAN.

I was a post-war hippy.

    NORMAN DAGLEY.

A drinking sort of person.

    ALEX HIGGINS.

I'M monosyllabic, if that's the word.

    STEVE DAVIS.

I'D be no good if I was placid. I need my intensity.

    ALEX HIGGINS.

I think he's great. He's got fewer zits than me and he's much better looking.

> STEPHEN HENDRY on his *Spitting Image* puppet.

Most of the top players these days are pretty characterless. And I was one of the first.

> STEVE DAVIS.

I'm a knockout merchant.

> PETER EBDON.

I'm afraid I'm one of these guys who wakes up singing and goes to bed dancing.

> BARRY HEARN.

You know these little model airplanes you can buy, and it flies into the wall. You fix it together with crazy glue and wonder if it's ever gonna fly again. Well, I'm like one of those. And it's gonna fly. It might fly kinda funny, but I kinda think it will.

> KIRK STEVENS.

You can call me the fastest of the slower players or the slowest of the faster players.

> CLIFF THORBURN.

As long as I'm not called a yuppie, I don't mind.

> STEPHEN HENDRY.

Everyone says I can't read or write, which is garbage. I can. I can get through the *Sporting Life* in about ten minutes.

> JIMMY WHITE.

As a matter of fact, apart from *Pot Black* in colour, it was the coming of the saviour, i.e. myself, that brought the game to public notice.

ALEX HIGGINS.

I'M pleased with the *Spitting Image* puppet of me – as it's so flattering. It makes me look better than I do in real life and I'm very proud of it.

STEVE DAVIS.

33
Sponsorship

Snooker Blood Money.

POSTER displayed by anti-smoking campaigner Stuart Holmes outside the Crucible Theatre each year during the World Championships sponsored by Embassy cigarettes.

It's important for a product like Bostik to have someone with a wholesome image. We have to be aware of the environment and of course there is the fact that we have solvent-based products that people abuse. Stephen fits the bill ideally.

RAY SCOTTING, sales and marketing manager, Bostik.

Desludging and effluent disposal services.

SLOGAN on Jim Chambers' car when he was sponsored by Processed Oils.

34
Success

I'VE shown a single-minded dedication which has been successful. People see it as un-British.

STEVE DAVIS.

STEVE Davis behaves as the British must behave if they are to maintain any position in the world. Order, method, discipline, plus a stern control of eccentricity, is the passport to triumph in the modern world.

BRIAN WALDEN, journalist and broadcaster.

IT'S funny. When I had nothing, I never used to worry about anything. But now I've got plenty of money and a fantastic lifestyle I worry all the time.

TONY MEO.

THE successful players are those who are fascinated by the game with all its intricacies.

JANICE HALE.

THE secret ingredients that go to make a sporting champion are the burning desire to succeed, the will to persevere, the vigour and dedication to cast aside all potential distractions and a love of the game. Hard work it may be, but to the player it must simply be a labour of love.

JOE DAVIS.

Success comes before work only in the dictionary.

JOHN VIRGO.

The one way to success at snooker is two-ball control; and two-ball control is utterly impossible until potting of the pottable ball is as automatic as is humanly possible.

JOE DAVIS.

When you are number one there is only one way to go – stay at number one.

BARRY HEARN.

You'll never be successful until you've learned to accept defeat.

MARIO BERNI.

The thing I noticed when I came on the circuit in 1985 was that there are really no bad players in the game. But equally I did recognise that there are so many players who are not prepared to apply themselves. Too many players with ability just want to sit and play cards, or spend their time in the bookie's or having fun. If you want success, you've got to be prepared to give these things up. You can appreciate players getting carried away with the glamour of the circuit. In the end, they become quite happy to knock up a result now and then, which is a tragedy.

IAN DOYLE.

35
Television

DALLAS with balls.

>BARRY HEARN on televised snooker.

SNOOKER helps boost our viewing figures but it damages the image of the channel. We will replace it with programmes for people who hate snooker.

>MICHAEL GRADE, Channel 4's chief executive, announcing his decision to drop snooker.

MOGADON sport.

>ADRIAN METCALFE, commissioning editor Channel 4.

SNOOKER would not have made it on television if it hadn't been for me. Without Hurricane excitement, the game would have gone its own mundane way.

>ALEX HIGGINS.

OUR fruit machine is the BBC. As soon as we sign that television contract, we are in clover.

>BARRY HEARN.

IT doesn't bother me really. Just occasionally, when I'm parking my little car among the Rolls Royces at Sheffield, I begin to wonder, but not for long.

>PHIL LEWIS, BBC producer and the originator of *Pot Black*.

It was like having a new baby.

>   NICK HUNTER, BBC producer, on the huge success of televised snooker.

It would be wrong to say we have killed it off. It is more a case of pronouncing the body dead.

>   ROY RONNIE, BBC information officer, announcing the end of *Pot Black*.

If they had to invent something to promote colour television they could not have thought of anything better than snooker.

>   JOHN SPENCER.

Do you know what really gets me? I've never played at my best in front of the TV cameras. People don't know just how good I am.

>   ALEX HIGGINS.

If snooker hadn't existed television would surely have had to invent it.

>   GEOFFREY NICHOLSON, journalist.

It turned all our cues into magic wands.

>   RAY REARDON.

The programme is full of nice-mannered people with smart bow-ties.

>   ELDERLY LADY praising *Pot Black*.

She wanted to stay to watch the end of Dennis's match against Jimmy White.

>   RUC SPOKESMAN explaining why Mrs Bridget Gervin had to be forcibly removed from her house minutes before a 1000 lb bomb demolished it. Mrs Gervin's family own the club in Coalisland where Dennis Taylor learned to play.

How about *Pot Black*? Does this curiously successful exhibition of professional snooker appeal to the sleazy denizens of the city billiards saloons, to the sporting gentlemen of London's clubland, or to both? Oddly enough, it has an even wider market. There is something immensely satisfying and restful about the game when seen in close-up and accompanied by an awed and whispered commentary. The viewer is there, on the spot, and the illusion is supported by the fact that the camera can stay put and does not need to wander hither and thither in pursuit of the action.

BERNARD HOLLOWOOD, journalist.

TV seems to create an image of people and I always seem to look miserable when I'm playing, so that's me. Mind you, Lester Piggott's done okay like that, hasn't he?

JOHN VIRGO.

POT BLACK is to other television sport as a string quartet is to a brass band.

PHILIP PURSER, television critic of the *Sunday Telegraph*.

THE real Upper Crusts are of course the gentlemen players of *Pot Black*, compered by 'Whispering' Ted Lowe. The snooker hall, once considered a small maelstrom of vulgarity, vice and, if you were lucky, purple sins, has been transformed by this series into a parlour of British refinement and gentility. It is here you will find the authentic murmur of Fair Play, and experience the sort of judiciously bottled-up excitement of the kind which in the old days could be trusted to distend a lady's bodice but without blowing a button. And by George, with those natty waistcoats, slick hair, and the restrained flamboyance of their bow ties, these princes of the green pelouse would not be out of place in some of our best tea shops. *Pot Black* even made a temporary gent of Hurricane Higgins last week; he of the ragged stroke and stupendous scoring.

PETER LENNON, journalist.

POT BLACK remains the only sports entertainment I really enjoy. The audience is more attentive than that for a string quartet. The players are so dapper in their waistcoats, immaculate shirts and bow ties; so straight in the back and dignified in their bearing – infinitely preferable to the hysterical pooves of the football field. Where else would the commentator (Ted Lowe) be able to speak without the need for player A to achieve a deep screw, Player B just to kiss the black and Player C to go in tight on the pink? Though as a reasonable good shot I must have had a good eye, the instant trigonometry, confidence and concentration of Fred Davis fill me with uncomprehending admiration.

PHILIP PURSER.

THIS is a pleasantly sleazy performance put across by Alan Weeks, who looks as though his misspent youth has never ended. A factor in its success is that no one cares who wins or loses. We all play shot by shot and the only winners are the balls.

'TACITUS', the *Belfast Sunday News* TV critic.

ALL of which gave the *Pot Black* final between Graham Miles and John Spencer, with the former homing to a breathtaking victory, an air of such civilised exchange that it emerged as almost the intellectual peak of the week.

MORNING STAR.

[SNOOKER] is something to do with sex, beautiful legs and bottoms, as medieval women may have enjoyed [jousting] tournaments and some women enjoy boxing.

A.S. BYATT, novelist.

... it's a combination of one to one dramatic human encounters with a geometric form both suited to the screen and to the watching imagination and memory.

IBID. Not many people know that.

36
Television Commentators

Yes, after eleven days, we're still as sharp as a button here.

DAVID VINE.

He won't feel the pressure as much as the more less-experienced players.

DAVID ICKE.

Steve Davis – acknowledged by his peers to be the peerless master.

JOHN MCCRIRICK.

There's no way he can't not go into the final session behind.

DENNIS TAYLOR.

He [Dene O'Kane] has really come out bristling on all cylinders.

JACK KARNEHM.

The butterflies are certainly flying around Higgins tonight.

TED LOWE.

He [John Parrott] has got three frames on the board, but bear in mind he's had to win them to get to that position.

JIM MEADOWCROFT.

WELL, it's almost impossible to miss, but hitting it is another matter.
    IBID.

As for you, I don't know about me, I'm ready for bed.
    DAVID VINE.

THE laughing Irish are smiling no longer.
    TED LOWE.

THE nerves are fluttering around in his tummy.
    TED LOWE.

TERRY now realises that the only way to win is to play well.
    JOHN SPENCER.

OF course, one of Stephen Hendry's greatest assets is his ability to score when he's playing.
    TED LOWE.

IF you didn't see Davis against Hendry last night, then you can see it again now.
    CHANNEL 4 presenter.

THE frame was one that could go either way but didn't.
    BBC COMMENTATOR.

WELL, we're back again tomorrow – all bright and bushy-eyed.

    DAVID VINE.

THEY'RE not only snooker players, they're engineers, taking apart a snooker cue and screwing it back again.

    TED LOWE.

NINETY-NINE times out of a thousand he would have potted that ball.

    TED LOWE.

THIS match has gradually and suddenly come to a climax.

    DAVID VINE.

HE's lucky in one sense and lucky in the other.

    TED LOWE.

OH, and that's a brilliant shot. The odd thing is his mum's not very keen on snooker.

    TED LOWE.

HIGGINS first entered the Championship ten years ago; that was for the first time, of course.

    TED LOWE.

JUST enough points here for Tony to pull the cat out of the fire.

    RAY EDMONDS.

AND it is my guess that Steve Davis will try to score as many points as he can in this frame.

    TED LOWE.

TONY Meo's beginning to find his potting boots.

    REX WILLIAMS.

SUDDENLY Alex Higgins was 7–0 down.

    DAVID VINE.

WHEN you start off it's nil–nil.

    STEVE DAVIS.

STEVE Davis has a tough consignment in front of him.

    TED LOWE.

FROM this position you've got to fancy either your opponent or yourself winning.

    KIRK STEVENS.

A little pale in the face, but then his name is White.

    TED LOWE.

THIS said, the inevitable failed to happen.

    JOHN PULMAN.

NO one came closer to winning the World title last year than the runner-up Dennis Taylor.

    DAVID VINE.

THAT puts the game beyond reproach.

TED LOWE.

HE'LL have no trouble in solving the solution.

JACK KARNEHM.

I'VE always said that the difference between winning and losing is nothing at all.

TERRY GRIFFITHS.

WELL, valour was the better part of discretion there.

JACK KARNEHM.

SOMETIMES the deciding frame's always the toughest to win.

DENNIS TAYLOR.

ALL square all the way round.

TED LOWE.

THERE is, I believe, a time limit for playing a shot. But I think it's true to say that nobody knows what that limit is.

IBID.

RAY Reardon, one of the great Crucible champions – won it five times when the championship was played away from the Crucible.

DAVID VINE.

JIMMY White has that wonderful gift of being able to point his cue where he is looking.

>   TED LOWE.

AND now snooker. And Steve Davis has crashed out of the UK Billiards Championship.

>   ALLAN TAYLOR.

WHEN you survey the plundering of this planet and the consequences screaming at us from each environmental report, introducing snooker, much as I enjoy it, takes on a new perspective.

>   DAVID ICKE, former snooker commentator and presently Son of God.

FRED Davis, the doyen of snooker, now sixty-seven years of age and too old to get his leg over, prefers to use his left hand.

>   TED LOWE having as much difficulty with his commentary as Davis was with his shot.

AND Alex Higgins has literally come back from the dead.

>   IBID.

IT's not easy to get a snooker when there's only one ball on the table.

>   IBID.

ONE mistake here could win or lose the match either way.

>   IBID.

CLIFF Thorburn has been unsettled by the erratic but consistent potting of Perrie Mans.

IBID.

PERRIE Mans played a prominent part in this tournament in 1979. In fact he won it.

IBID.

THE audience are literally electrified and glued to their seats.

IBID.

AND for those of you watching this in black and white, the pink sits behind the yellow.

IBID.

10–4 . . . and it could mean exactly what that means.

DAVID VINE.

AFTER twelve frames they stand all square. The next frame, believe it or not, is the thirteenth.

IBID.

BUT there was still the big prize money hanging there like a carrot waiting to be picked.

IBID.

I'M speaking from a deserted and virtually empty Crucible Theatre.

IBID.

HERE we are in the Holy Land of Israel, a Mecca for tourists.

IBID.

JIMMY can make these balls talk, and what a story they're telling.

>TED LOWE on Jimmy White.

AND Griffiths has looked at that blue four times now and it still hasn't moved.

>IBID.

THAT's inches away from being millimetre perfect.

>IBID.

JOHN Smyth is getting his little implement out.

>TED LOWE on referee Smyth.

THERE he is, 20 stone of Canadian fat.

>TED LOWE on Bill Werbeniuk, who was displeased not least because he claimed to be only 19 stone.

HE's got within Jimmy's girth.

>JOHN VIRGO.

HURRICANE Higgins can either win or lose this final match tomorrow.

>ARCHIE MCPHERSON.

A two-frame lead is really only one.

>EDDIE CHARLTON.

HE made a break of 98, which was almost one hundred.

>ALAN WEEKS.

This of course is a shot that Ray's an expert at ... that's seven points away.

TED LOWE.

It's at times like these that you have to clench your teeth together and say a prayer.

TED LOWE.

When he [Alex Higgins] has got his tail up, he's a very hard nut to crack.

JACK KARNEHM.

And that's the third time he's done that this session. He's missed his waistcoat pocket with the chalk.

TED LOWE.

Can Bill Werbeniuk be the second Canadian to rewrite the history books?

IBID.

This young man Jimmy White celebrated his twenty-second birthday literally four days ago.

IBID.

John Spencer can't really afford to be 5–1 down at such an early stage.

JACK KARNEHM.

Alex, unlike many other professionals, adds a bit on his cue rather than put on an extension.

TED LOWE.

He's 40 points behind and there's only 51 points left on the table.

IBID.

That cue arm, now in perfect rhythm with his thinking.

JOHN PULMAN.

Steve, with his sip of water, part of his make-up.

TED LOWE.

The audience is standing to relieve themselves.

TED LOWE.

Well, the shot would have been safe if the red hadn't ended up over the pocket.

IBID.

Steve Davis is trailing by one frame, so the pressure is balanced on him.

REX WILLIAMS.

He's obviously worked out for himself that he doesn't need that last red . . . great thinker this man.

DENNIS TAYLOR.

And Jimmy's potting literally doing the commentary here.

TED LOWE.

He's completely disappeared. He's gone back to his dressing room. Nobody knows where he has gone.

TED LOWE.

WE do still get letters about 'kicks'. There's no explanation. It's a little piece of dirt on the cue ball.

DENNIS TAYLOR.

IT all adds up to a bit of fun. If commentators can't join in with the rest of the world, they must cry alone.

TED LOWE.

COMMENTATING isn't as simple as it sounds.

IBID.

SOMETIMES silence is golden.

IBID.

37
Winning

WE'RE only interested in the top-of-the-world stuff. We're not interested in the grassroots, in the near-greats and also-rans. It's all about winning. You've got to be a winner or you're nothing.

BARRY HEARN.

I know how to win and with enough bullets in me I can do it quite easily. Some people are never winners, don't have the awareness required to get to the finishing line. But that's not my problem. Possibly familiarity with the winning post means that you do soften up a bit.

STEVE DAVIS on his loss of form in recent seasons.

WINNERS win. Losers make their own arrangements.

SNOOKER saying.

I'VE had some hostility now and then but one of the hard facts of life about living in Britain is that the public don't like winners.

STEPHEN HENDRY.

STEPHEN has no idea what he has let himself in for. As long as he wins he will be hated, reviled even, and he's got to ignore that.

BARRY HEARN on Stephen Hendry.

SINCE Steve has lost a few matches, he's developed charisma and he's a national hero.

BARRY HEARN on Steve Davis.

I like to win in a special way. I like to show what can be done if you really think about it. That's why I can fill a hall at 11 a.m. on a wet morning in Sheffield.

> ALEX HIGGINS.

We live in a tabloid society and people are looking for someone new all the time. Results are the only thing that don't lie.

> BARRY HEARN.

I felt really gutted for Alex because he's my hero and I really only came along to get some experience.

> NEAL FOULDS after his 10–9 victory over Alex Higgins during the 1984 Embassy World Championship.

You have to take total responsibility for winning. It's never fate. It's always you.

> KIRK STEVENS.

I've never been so chuffed in my life, not even winning the World Championship.

> TERRY GRIFFITHS after his son Wayne won the Llanelli and District Championship.

I wanted to cry for him. It was the biggest day of my life but it was pitiful to see his face.

> TERRY GRIFFITHS on his 13–12 victory over Alex Higgins in the 1979 Embassy World Championship. He went on to win the title.

I feel numb. I feel more emotional than when I lost. I expected to feel different.

> GARY WILKINSON after defeating Steve Davis in the final of the 1991 Coalite World Matchplay.

I can't remember anyone ever asking 'Who came second?' Can you?

>RAY REARDON.

As they say in boxing, you have to knock your man out in Australia to get a draw.

>IBID.

IF you can keep playing the balls, forget your opponent and forget about the products of winning, then you can be a winner.

>DENNIS TAYLOR.

I love winning, but then it's only a game. We will be presenting some wheelchairs to some unlucky kids after this championship. That puts everything into perspective.

>IBID.

IF I don't win I don't eat.

>BOB CHAPERON.

BY the way, I know how to beat Steve Davis.

>STEPHEN HENDRY to his manager Ian Doyle a few weeks after Davis had beaten him six times in six nights during a tour of Scotland.

REACHING the final was like swimming the Channel, but winning it is like swimming the Atlantic.

>DOUG MOUNTJOY on his win over Stephen Hendry in the final of the 1988 Tennents UK Open.

To beat the other man. To beat him as utterly, as completely as possible. This was the deep and abiding meaning of the game of pool. And, it seemed to Eddie in that minute of thought, it was the meaning of more than the game of pool, more than the five-by-ten microcosm of ambition and desire. It seemed to him as if all men must know this because it is in every meeting and every act, in the whole gigantic hustle of men's lives.

FROM *The Hustler* by Walter Tevis.

38

Women Players

WHEN I beat a man at pool he seems to think he's had his willy chopped off.

>   SUE THOMPSON.

THEY tell me a woman can't play properly because of her shape... I tell them it hasn't stopped Bill Werbeniuk.

>   ALLISON FISHER.

SHE is good, but there are 122 better. It seems like sex discrimination in reverse. Maybe we should all start dressing in drag.

>   JOHN SHILTON on plans to allow Allison Fisher to join the professional snooker circuit as a special case.

IT will be disgusting if they let her in.

>   DENNIS STEVESON, manager of Stefan Mazrocis, on the same issue. Later the professional circuit was thrown open to all, regardless of standard.

ONCE in Northern Ireland, a man gave me flowers as if to commiserate with me for losing before we'd even started. I hit him with a 50 break and then slaughtered him.

>   ALLISON FISHER.

They tell me a woman can't play properly because of her shape . . . I tell them it hasn't stopped Bill Werbeniuk

I don't want it said that we've only picked the best-looking girls. The last thing I want is the women's liberation front round my neck with all the feminist nonsense. We're trying to do something for the women as well.

> BARRY HEARN responding to complaints that good-looking rather than the best women snooker players were picked to appear in a televised competition.

THIS is not sex discrimination as far as we are concerned. The snooker room has always been a men's room. This is a working men's club and women members are only half-members. A woman is not a full member in her own right.

> LES RANDALL, secretary of the Wakefield City Working Men's Club, rejecting claims by member Sheila Capstick that she had been banned from the snooker tables because she had become too good for the men.

IT is archaic. Those pompous little men are just living in the Dark Ages. Their attitude is truly pathetic when you consider we have a woman Prime Minister. If it was not for the principle involved, we would have a good laugh.

> TERESA BURNELL, who, with her friend Sue Jones, was banned for a year from the Otteshaw Social Club for playing snooker.

RAVING husbands and boyfriends are never off the phone to me now. Many complain that they've been left no dinner. Others say they are just lonely.

> COACH BRIAN HALTER, founder and president of the Bristol Ladies Billiard and Snooker Association, after more than a hundred women took up his offer of coaching lessons.

They say there really should not be
A difference at all
Between the men and women
Who address a snooker ball.
It takes no special strength they say
To play at stun and screw
And really it's quite graceful
To perform with billiard cue.
But 'they' were wrong as Vera found
When taking up the game
And women are at a disadvantage
They're just not the same.
She sallied forth one evening
To play against a man
In quite a major snooker match,
And proceeded with her plan
To baffle him with safety play
Pot every ball with care.
It all began to pay off fine,
He was showing signs of wear
The vital ball to clinch the game
Was there for her to pot.
The atmosphere was very tense,
Opponent very hot.
She played with screw to pot the black
Would it drop in? – just!
But the referee called out 'foul stroke'
The white ball touched your bust.

VERA SELBY

WE feel snooker is a man's game. We feel that if a man wants to give vent to his feelings, he should not have to look over his shoulder before he does so. This rule is to stop women hearing bad language.

CHARLES DANDY, secretary of the Smethwick Working Men's Club, defending the banning of women spectators.

The Sexiest Game in Town

I wonder why it is
That so few women play the game
Even when the opportunity
To play's the same?
I've thought about it often,
It's a question that can vex,
And I think it is because
The game of Snooker's full of sex!
Well, all those balls to start with
And then what about the cue?
A phallic symbol there's no doubt,
Thrusting towards you.
Then, in a game when bending forward,
Potting on your mind,
The referee calls loud and clear the score
And 'Striker behind!'
'You want to get more bottom on,'
They constantly are saying,
And 'Watch it, or you'll get a kiss'
They tell you while you're playing.
'It's such a shame' you hear them say,
When everything's gone wrong,
'You're lying on the cushion,
And you've simply nothing on!'
But worst of all, please tell me
What exactly do you do
When a fellow sidles up and asks
'Just how well can you screw?'

VERA SELBY

IF blokes call me rubbish I don't argue with them – I just demolish them on the pool table.

SUE THOMPSON. Thompson took the Professional Pool Players' Organisation to an industrial tribunal when she was not allowed to join. The tribunal found she had been a victim of sexual discrimination and gave the Organisation three months to grant her professional status.

39
World Championships

I went into my local club when I got back home, somewhere I played every day, and did what I always did, put my name up on the board. And they go, 'Oh, look at this boys, the world champion here's put his name up on the board. I'm not coming off the table to let the world champion on.' And it just went through my fuckin' heart. I never went to the club again. Never. Although it's still in my town. I couldn't accept it, you see. They all changed towards me in a day.

> TERRY GRIFFITHS relating his experiences on his visit to his local club after winning the World Championship.

THE Championship was my passport to carnal pleasure.

> ALEX HIGGINS on the unexpected consequences of winning the World Championship in 1972.

THE biggest buzz, the greatest excitement in life for me is practice at a snooker table. That beats sex, love, romance. . . . I'm sorry to sound so cold, but unless you've tasted the thrill of being in the World Championships, you'll find me difficult to understand.

> STEVE DAVIS.

IT wasn't difficult, but it wasn't easy.

> STEVE DAVIS on his failure to pot the last black in the final frame of the 1985 World Championship against Dennis Taylor.

A bit of a match that.

> DENNIS TAYLOR after he potted the black and became world champion.

WHEN those curtains open, it does my brains in.

> STEVE LONGWORTH on walking into the arena at the Embassy World Championship.

I always drive into Sheffield the day before the tournament starts, just to get the flavour. It's something I do every year. As soon as I see the Crucible, my stomach starts churning over. The butterflies have arrived.

> STEVE DAVIS.

THE Crucible is about surviving the agonies and the whole traumas of the whole Championship and keep coming back for more. It's about still being strong at the end.

> IBID.

IN sixty years there's never been a champion who won the world title on ability alone. You have to harness that ability.

> JACK KARNEHM.

I'M in the final now, you know.

> TERRY GRIFFITHS after winning against Eddie Charlton in the semi-final of the 1979 Embassy World Championship.

IT was like Sergeant Bilko beating Ali over the full fifteen.

> FRANK KEATING, journalist, on Dennis Taylor's win over Steve Davis in the 1985 Embassy World Championship final.

I'M over the moon. It's like the comics I used to read. I don't know how I do it.

> JOE JOHNSON after defeating Neal Foulds 16–9 to reach the 1987 Embassy World Championship final.

It's so difficult to win this and it takes so much out of you that you have to be prepared for anything. You never know when you're going to fall apart.

> STEVE DAVIS after beating Joe Johnson in the 1987 Embassy World Championship final.

I like playing in Sheffield . . . it's full of melancholy happy-go-lucky people.

> ALEX HIGGINS.

It was a Crucible collywobble.

> STEVE DAVIS after his first-round win over John Virgo in the 1988 Embassy World Championship.

CRUCIBLE – any severe test or trial, vessel made to endure great heat, a melting pot, a furnace.

> *SHORTER OXFORD ENGLISH DICTIONARY*

In the beginning it felt like Steve and me against the world. We'd sit up late into the night dreaming about what we'd do when we won the World Championship. It was like the search for the Holy Grail, and when we made it three years later it was one of the greatest moments of my life.

> BARRY HEARN.

I owe it to the game, because of all the joy the game's given me.

> JIMMY WHITE explaining why he feels winning the World Championship is so important.

THE lights of the Crucible dim. The shuffling in the audience dies away and there is a sort of respectful silence you would normally expect for some celebrated chamber music quartet. It is a very gentlemanly atmosphere, heightened by the black waistcoats, white shirts and black ties the players wear as uniform, and respected by the audience whose comments never rose above a whisper. Even the whispers die away eventually so that the darkened auditorium is almost silent except for the snicking of the snooker balls and the referee's calling the score. I didn't actually nod off but came as close to complete relaxation as I thought possible. Why it should be labelled a working-class sport is beyond me. For the tired, harassed business executive I can think of no better way of relaxing.

>JOURNALIST, *Morning Telegraph*.

I felt very loose, very good for the final session. I felt very tall as if I could look at the table from above.

>CLIFF THORBURN describing his experience when winning the 1980 Embassy World Championship.

I'M not going to the Crucible for the experience. I don't expect to lose.

>PETER EBDON, who did lose but not before he knocked out Steve Davis in the 1992 Embassy World Championship.

I managed to get my nose in front and with a nose like mine that's a big lead.

>MICK PRICE, No. 82 in the world, after beating Dennis Taylor in the 1992 Embassy World Championships.

I can't feel gutted because Stephen played like God.

>JIMMY WHITE after losing the 1992 Embassy World Championship final to Stephen Hendry.

I was so nervous going into the arena I could just see myself falling down the stairs. They should get a banister there for newcomers.

>MICK PRICE on his debut at the Crucible.

PLAYING Jimmy White in the semi-finals of the World Championships, it seems crazy. A couple of years ago I was a million miles away from where I am now. It's a dream.

ALAN MCMANUS.

NOW I can die happy.

ALEX HIGGINS after winning the 1982 Embassy World Championship.

THERE was a special feeling about the place. I knew this was my home. I imagined it full, the buzz, the excitement, everything. I wanted it all for myself.

PETER EBDON'S first impressions of the Crucible the day before he made his debut there.

AFTER winning the World Championship once, Terryl and I didn't think we'd like to win it again.

JOE JOHNSON on the price of fame.

THE Marathon of the Mind.

ANONYMOUS.

THE Tour de France without a bike.

ANONYMOUS.

40
Youth

It was villains I used to know in the early days, villains and thieves to tell the truth, but they were good to me, never harmed their own.

    JIMMY WHITE.

Today's youngsters play snooker as if they are having open-heart surgery.

    CLIFF WILSON.

Playing for 25 cents in a bad part of town was how you grew up.

    CLIFF THORBURN.

Kids are better off in a snooker hall than running about vandalising tower blocks.

    ALEX HIGGINS.

When I was fifteen, I looked twelve, so when this little wimp went up to somebody and said, 'I'd like to play for $500', they thought they couldn't lose. . . . I was beaten up a few times, black eyes and stuff like that.

    KIRK STEVENS.

There was a snooker hall across the road where I spent time away from my lessons. I found a lot of comradeship there, a lot of friendship. It helped me to come to terms with being part of a new society.

    BILL MORRIS, general secretary of the Transport and General Workers' Union. Originally from Jamaica, he was studying at college in Birmingham.

I know they expect the best tables, the best of everything. That's not the way to learn. They don't know what it's like to play for threepence with tuppence in their pocket.

ALEX HIGGINS.

THERE'S something wrong with a young chap who doesn't play games. Not even snooker.

BERNARD HOLLOWOOD, *Scowle in the Sixties*.

I would have got into real trouble if it hadn't been for snooker.

CLIFF THORBURN.

THE new kids are all good players but they are all the same, they have no personality.

TERRY GRIFFITHS.

IT'S true – snooker saved me from being a plonker. When I was sixteen, I was a complete idiot. I was sixteen going on twelve. And I behaved like people wanted to smash me in the face. I was reasonably intelligent, but I was a complete nonentity. If I didn't turn up for a lesson, nobody would even notice, and I can't blame them.

STEVE DAVIS.

SNOOKER saved my youth. It took me off the streets.

TERRY GRIFFITHS.

I don't regret anything – you're only young once and you can't buy youth.

JOE O'BOYE.

I had already decided to concentrate on snooker when I left school. I took eight O levels but would have needed to go back to school to find out the results. I didn't bother.

BARRY WEST.

He has a flair for living. When he was twelve he was as worldly as a forty-year-old and as naive as a four-year-old. Jimmy would work out a Yankee, but couldn't name the capital of France.

BARRY HEARN on Jimmy White.

It may raise the odd titter, but I genuinely want snooker to lose its misspent youth image and become as honorable as golf or cricket.

ALEX HIGGINS.

We never knew where we would be going next, tournaments, challenges, anything. We used to iron our money. If you had £50 then, that was a lot of money, so we used to look after it, crease it, you know. We just played. We just loved it. Getting a few pounds here and there and suddenly we were wearing suits. It overtook us really. We never thought the game was going to be this big.

JIMMY WHITE.

The responsibility will be his alone if the next generation of kids turns out to be nicotine-stained, hollow-cheeked, ashen-faced and thin as a bootlace.

WILLIAM MARSHALL, journalist, on Alex Higgins.

We used to iron our money. If you had £50 then, that was a lot of money, so we used to look after it, crease it, you know

41
Final Word

It's better than working.

> TERRY GRIFFITHS.

If I'm remembered for anything at all, I'd like it to be as the man who put the smile back into snooker.

> DENNIS TAYLOR.

Anything's better than pouring someone's cold Sunday dinner over your head.

> DANNY FOWLER, a former dustman.

If it wasn't hard, what would be the point of doing it?

> STEVE DAVIS.

I spent over fifty years in the game. It was very lucrative, very enjoyable but terribly exacting. And in the end, it was enough.

> JOE DAVIS.

Never forget that enjoyment is the key to it all. It certainly has been for me.

> FRED DAVIS.

It's better than digging.

> JOE JOHNSON, a former British Gas labourer.

Snooker is not life or death. It's only a game.

RAY REARDON.

Sure I want to make some money. I think I will. But the game's more important than any of us. If we can do things which will make the game bigger, everybody will benefit.

CLIFF THORBURN.

The things I always try to do are to play the game well and leave a good impression wherever I go.

EDDIE CHARLTON.

It is a game with universal appeal and I hope that one day every lad and every girl of every nationality will have the chance to climb out of the pits to the top of the world.

RAY REARDON.

I don't think about what might have been if I'd been born later. I don't think I could have had a better life. Everything is relative. I remember working 130 hours in the paper mill and getting £30, so I appreciate what snooker has done for me.

JOHN SPENCER.

Index

Acteson, Steve, 65, 66
Alderton, John, 92
Allen, Fred, 97
Almey, David, 68
Alverston, Lord, 16
Amin, Idi, 15
Amis, Martin, 85
Antony and Cleopatra, 24

Balsis, Joe, 76
Barbarito, Archbishop, 90
Barnes, Simon, 17
Barry, John, 23
Belfast Sunday News, 124
Benson & Hedges Irish Masters, **1985**, 95 **1992**, 56
Benson & Hedges Masters, **1984**, 12, 13 **1988**, 16 **1990**, 52 **1991**, 104
Berni, Mario, 120
Best, George, 17
Billiards & Snooker, 41
Billiards Association and Control Council, 34
Billiards Championship, 1919, 16
Borg, Bjorn, 84
Brazier, Robbo, 20, 108
Bridge, Anthony, 59
British Board of Censors, 97
British Car Rental World Cup, 1990, 14
British Migraine Association, 46
Broadhurst, Terry, 81
Brown, Alec, 34
Brown, Councillor Jack, 79
Burnell, Teresa, 142
Burnley Evening Star, 81
Burrows, John, 88
Butera, Lou, 76
Byatt, A.S., 124

Callan, Frank, 50, 51, 55, 85, 87
Canadian Dick, 86
Capstick, Sheila, 142
Carson, Frank, 15
Castle Snooker Club, Leicester, 68
Chamberlain, Col. Sir Neville, 8
Chambers, Charles, 34
Chambers, Jim, 118
Chaperon, Bob, 138
Charlton, Eddie, 15, 17, 74, 80, 94, 96, 114, 132, 146, 156
Chas 'n' Dave, 79
Clover, Ron, 82
Coalite World Matchplay, **1991**, 138
Color of Money, The, 71, 78, 98, 99
Coral UK Open, **1984**, 109
Corbett, Ted, 79
Cotton, Charles, 24
Crane, Irving, 76
Crawley, Alfred E., 26
Cripsey, Graham, 77, 88
Crucible, 84, 118, 129, 131, 146, 147, 148, 149
Cruise, Tom, 78

Dagley, Norman, 24, 51, 80, 115
Daily Telegraph, 90
Dandy, Charles, 143
Davis, Bill, 78
Davis, Fred, 12, 27, 33, 39, 43, 45, 51, 75, 92, 93, 100, 102, 110, 115, 124, 130, 154
Davis, Jean, 77
Davis, Joe, 12, 24, 28, 29, 41, 51, 66, 71, 72, 73, 78, 85, 90, 91, 94, 95, 96, 103, 114, 119, 120, 154
Davis, Steve, 9, 15, 19, 20, 26, 31, 33, 36, 49, 50, 52, 54, 55, 56, 57, 58, 59, 64, 65, 67, 68, 69, 72, 75, 77, 79, 81,

82, 84, 86, 87, 88, 91, 93, 95, 97, 101, 102, 103, 104, 105, 109, 112, 113, 114, 116, 117, 119, 126, 127, 128, 129, 133, 134, 136, 139, 145, 146, 147, 151, 154
Dennison, Stephen, 97
Diffley, Mrs I. E., 42
Doyle, Ian, 19, 37, 40, 60, 61, 69, 82, 100, 120, 139
Drago, Tony, 75
Driffield, Leslie, 27
Dulux British Open, **1986**, 54
Dunning, John, 51

Ebdon, Peter, 108, 116, 148, 149
Edmonds, Ray, 93, 127
Egan, Sir John, 30
Embassy World Championship, 106, 118, 145, 146, 147, 149 **1979**, 137, 146 **1980**, 148 **1981**, 14 **1982**, 93, 94, 149 **1983**, 9, 16, 19, 54, 77 **1984**, 52, 137 **1985**, 145, 146 **1986**, 52 **1987**, 103, 109, 112, 146, 147 **1988**, 54, 147 **1989**, 54 **1990**, 16 **1992**, 11, 148 **1993**, 45
Everton, Clive, 14, 29, 30, 39, 88, 94, 97, 105, 108

Fagan, Patsy, 63
Faithfull, Marianne, 21
Fast Eddie Felson, 82, 98
Ferreira, Michael, 51
Fidelity International, **1987**, 88 **1988**, 81, 86, 114
Fisher, Allison, 56, 57, 73, 140
Foulds, Neal, 15, 39, 40, 54, 56, 75, 137, 146
'Four Away', 79
Fowler, Danny, 154
Foxley, Roland, 28
Francisco, Mannie, 11, 51
Freer, Roy, 86
Fricker, Brenda, 92

Ganley, Len, 74, 110, 111
Gervin, Mrs Bridget, 122
Gilbert, William S., 27
Glasgow School of Motivation, 60
Gold, Sir Arthur, 39
Grade, Michael, 121
Gray, George, 27, 74
Green, Geoffrey, 28
Griffiths, Martin, 16

Griffiths, Terry, 21, 47, 54, 57, 58, 69, 70, 79, 86, 96, 106, 109, 113, 129, 137, 145, 146, 151, 154
Griffiths, Wayne, 137
Gross, Ron, 55
Guildford, David, 93

Hale, Janice, 47, 51, 65, 88, 119
Half Man Half Biscuit, 111
Hallett, Mike, 104
Halter, Brian, 142
Harper, Ronnie, 80
Harrows' Leisure Centre, 92
Hearn, Barry, 9, 17, 20, 50, 59, 60, 61, 63, 69, 70, 72, 78, 80, 82, 86, 88, 96, 100, 103, 106, 114, 116, 120, 121, 136, 137, 142, 147, 152
Helmstetter, Richard, 90
Hendry, Stephen, 17, 19, 31, 37, 60, 70, 82, 86, 87, 88, 91, 95, 104, 105, 116, 118, 126, 136, 139, 148
Hennessey, Christian, 22
Higgins, Alex, 9, 14, 15, 16, 17, 19, 22, 24, 31, 33, 35, 36, 40, 42, 45, 48, 49, 51, 54, 55, 63, 65, 67, 68, 76, 77, 79, 80, 81, 82, 84, 85, 87, 93, 94, 97, 110, 112, 113, 114, 116, 117, 121, 122, 123, 127, 128, 130, 132, 133, 137, 145, 147, 149, 150, 151, 152
Hollowood, Bernard, 123, 151
Holmes, Stuart, 118
Houlihan, Pat, 90
Hughes, Eugene, 95
Hunn, David, 28, 86
Hunter, Nick, 122
Hustler, The, 82, 95, 96, 139

Icke, David, 125, 130
Inman, Melbourne, 16, 22, 44, 74

Jackson, George, 63
Jackson, Judge David, 63
James, Clive, 78, 79, 84, 90
John Courage English Professional Championship, **1981**, 93
Johnson, Joe, 11, 146, 147, 149, 154
Jones, Sue, 142
Jonson, Ben, 27

Karnehm, Jack, 11, 23, 26, 35, 94, 125, 129, 133, 146

Keating, Frank, 146
King, Billie-Jean, 84
King Edward VII, 92
Kipling, Rudyard, 29
Kirkwood, Geordie, 93
Knowles, Tony, 16, 36, 74, 79
Kruger, Howard, 63, 77

Lada Cars Classic, **1982**, 9
Lafir, Mohammed, 50
Lassiter, Luther, 98
Lennon, Peter, 123
Levin, Angela, 79
Lewis, Phil, 121
Lindrum, Walter, 78
Longworth, Steve, 109, 146
Lowe, Ted, 41, 71, 75, 84, 123, 124, 125, 126, 127, 128, 129, 130, 131, 132, 133, 134, 135
Lucas, E. V., 24

Mans, Perrie, 74, 88, 130
Marshall, William, 152
Mazrocis, Stefan, 140
Meadowcroft, Jim, 125, 126
Meo, Tony, 52, 79, 94, 119, 127
Mercantile Credit Classic, **1987**, 55 **1988**, 97
Metcalfe, Adrian, 121
Miles, Graham, 124
Miller-Cheevers, Noel, 60, 61
Minnesota Fats, 82, 98
Moran, Kevin, 86
Morning Star, 124
Morning Telegraph, 148
Morris, Bill, 150
Mother John Baptist, 90
Mountjoy, Doug, 22, 28, 43, 50, 139
Moynihan, Colin, 39
Murphy, Stephen, 85

McCririck, John, 125
McEnroe, John, 84
McGoorty, Danny, 98
McIlvanney, Hugh, 91, 104, 105
McLoughlin, John, 68
McManus, Alan, 149
McPherson, Archie, 132

Nastase, Ilie, 84
Newman, Paul, 78

Newman, Tom, 34
New York Fats, 48
Nicholson, Ben, 29
Nicholson, Geoffrey, 122
Novick, Alison, 39

O'Boye, Joe, 151
O'Kane, Dene, 41, 50, 125
Owen, Gary, 55

Parris, John, 33
Parrott, John, 52, 54, 55, 97, 106, 115, 125
Patmore, Angela, 105
Peall, W. J., 74
Pearl Assurance British Open, **1991**, 52, 85 **1992**, 11
Pepys, Samuel, 26
Pontins Open, 21 **1978**, 69
Pot Black, 68, 121, 122, 123, 124
Price, Mick, 148
Priestley, J. B., 80
Priestley, Raymond, 90
Princess Royal, 92
Private Eye, 84
Processed Oils, 118
Professional Pool Players' Organisation, 144
Pugh, Sheenagh, 13
Pulman, John, 17, 43, 44, 92, 96, 115, 128, 134
PULSE, 46
Purser, Philip, 123, 124

Randall, Les, 142
Randle, Colin, 16
Rea, Jackie, 74
Reardon, Ray, 12, 17, 21, 31, 33, 34, 42, 45, 59, 64, 69, 70, 73, 84, 85, 88, 122, 129, 138, 156
Reece, Tom, 16, 77
Reynolds, Dean, 52, 67
Roberts, John Jnr, 87
Robidoux, Alain, 81
Ronnie, Roy, 122
Ross, Chris, 90
Rothmans Grand Prix, **1988**, 54 **1989**, 52, **1991**, 68

Scotting, Ray, 118
Scowle in the Sixties, 151

INDEX

Selby, Vera, 143, 144
Shakespeare, William, 24
Shaw, Darren, 110
Shilton, John, 140
Silver, Eric, 26
Simmons, Del, 67
Sinatra, Frank, 86
Skidmore, Norman, 55
Smethwick Working Men's Club, 143
Smith, Willie, 24
Smyth, John, 132
Snooker Scene, 14, 39, 42, 67, 77
South Yorkshire County Council, 79
Spencer, Herbert, 23
Spencer, John, 9, 12, 31, 46, 50, 75, 86, 87, 108, 122, 124, 126, 133, 156
Spencer on Snooker, 50
Spitting Image, 72, 116, 117
Sports Council's Drug Abuse Group, 39
Stevens, Kirk, 12, 13, 38, 43, 45, 52, 70, 75, 79, 81, 106, 109, 116, 128, 137, 150
Steveson, Dennis, 140
Sunday Telegraph, 123
Super Crystalate United Kingdom Championships, **1977**, 22

'Tacitus', 124
Tart, Mandy, 37
Taylor, Allan, 130
Taylor, David, 78
Taylor, Dennis, 14, 21, 28, 70, 79, 80, 81, 114, 122, 125, 129, 134, 135, 138, 145, 146, 148, 154
Tennents UK Open, **1987**, 11, 56 **1988**, 50, 139
Tevis, Walter, 71, 95, 96, 98, 99, 139
Thompson, Sue, 140, 144
Thorburn, Cliff, 9, 11, 12, 14, 44, 47, 72, 78, 86, 88, 91, 105, 106, 112, 116, 130, 148, 150, 151, 156
Thorn, A. Stanley, 78
Thorne, Willie, 11, 19, 37, 54, 74, 79, 103, 108, 113
Thurston's Hall, 80
Trelford, Donald, 81
Twain, Mark, 28

UK Billiards Championship, 129

Valdimarsson, Brynjar, 86
Vicious, Sid, 17
Vine, David, 125, 126, 128, 129, 131
Virgo, Avril, 37
Virgo, John 85, 104, 108, 120, 123, 132, 147

Wakefield City Working Men's Club, 142
Walden, Brian, 119
Wall, Muriel, 46
Walsh, John, 50
Wattana, James, 9, 11, 70, 82, 108, 115
Watterson, Mike, 60, 61, 63
Weeks, Alan, 124, 132
Welch, Julie, 81
Wenham, Brian, 23
Werbeniuk, Bill, 46, 47, 65, 78, 88, 132, 133, 140
West, Barry, 152
Weston, Jason, 52
White, Jimmy, 11, 12, 50, 51, 56, 71, 73, 79, 81, 90, 96, 114, 117, 122, 129, 132, 133, 147, 148, 149, 150, 152
Wigglesworth, D., 77
Wilkinson, Gary, 138
Williams, Rex, 11, 38, 39, 45, 67, 91, 92, 100, 128, 134
Williamson, Ian, 110
Willis, Don, 98
Wilson, Cliff, 17, 20, 54, 150
Wilton, Ann, 67
Wise, Dorothy, 26
World Amateur Billiards Championship, **1971**, 80
World Championship, 114, **1972**, 55, 145 **1973**, 17 **1978**, 90
World Cup, **1980**, 78
World Masters, 9
WPBSA, 67, 100, 112
Wright, Jon, 68, 75
Wych, Jim, 103

Yamaha International Masters, **1984**, 51
Young, Judge Christopher, 68